DATE DUE

MIDDLE EAST NATIONS IN THE NEWS

Israel
IN THE NEWS

PAST, PRESENT, AND FUTURE

David Aretha

MyReportLinks.com Books
an imprint of

 Enslow Publishers, Inc. **E**
Box 398, 40 Industrial Road
Berkeley Heights, NJ 07922
USA

MyReportLinks.com Books, an imprint of Enslow Publishers, Inc. MyReportLinks®
is a registered trademark of Enslow Publishers, Inc.

Library of Congress Cataloging-in-Publication Data

Aretha, David.
 Israel in the news : past, present, and future / David Aretha.
     p. cm. — (Middle East nations in the news)
 Includes bibliographical references and index.
 ISBN 1-59845-028-X
 1. Israel—Juvenile literature. 2. Jews—History—Juvenile literature. 3. Arab-Israeli conflict—
1993— –Peace—Juvenile literature. I. Title. II. Series.
 DS102.95.A75 2006
 956.9405—dc22

                                    2005030698

Printed in the United States of America

10 9 8 7 6 5 4 3 2 1

To Our Readers:
Through the purchase of this book, you and your library gain access to the Report Links that specifically
back up this book.
The Publisher will provide access to the Report Links that back up this book and will keep these Report
Links up to date on **www.myreportlinks.com** for five years from the book's first publication date.
We have done our best to make sure all Internet addresses in this book were active and appropriate when
we went to press. However, the author and the Publisher have no control over, and assume no liability for,
the material available on those Internet sites or on other Web sites they may link to.
The usage of the MyReportLinks.com Books Web site is subject to the terms and conditions stated on
the Usage Policy Statement on **www.myreportlinks.com.**
A password may be required to access the Report Links that back up this book. The password is found on
the bottom of page 4 of this book.
Any comments or suggestions can be sent by e-mail to comments@myreportlinks.com or to the address
on the back cover.

Photo Credits: AP/Wide World Photos, pp. 1, 94, 98; *Atlas of the Middle East,* Central Intelligence
Agency, pp. 20, 90; Bureau of Public Affairs, U.S. Department of State, p. 105; Central Intelligence Agency,
pp. 6 (map), 56, 58, 60–61, 63, 65; © BBC MMV, pp. 10, 75, 103; © BBC 2002–05, p. 26; © Corel
Corporation, pp. 3, 6, 13, 22, 33, 35, 39, 42–43, 50–51, 54, 67, 70–71, 80, 107, 112–113; © 5756–5763
(1995–2002), Tracey R. Rich, p. 49; © 1995–2005 wgbh educational foundation, p. 99; © 1996, Richard
Hooker, p. 32; © The Israel Museum, Jerusalem, 1995–2005, p. 30; © 2005 Time, Inc., p. 47; © 2004
The State of Israel, pp. 21, 86; © 2005 Cable News Network, LP, LLLP, p. 81; © 2005 Educational
Broadcasting Corporation, p. 92; © 2005 ESPN Internet Ventures, p. 66; © 2005 Israel Defense Forces,
p. 88; © 2005 Israel Ministry of Tourism, p. 109; © 2005 LIFE, Inc., p. 37; © 2005 Prime Minister's Office,
p. 96; © 2005 The American-Israeli Cooperative Enterprise, pp. 23, 111 ; © 2005 The American Israel
Public Affairs Committee, p. 12; © 2005, The State of Israel, p. 44; © 2005 WN Network, p. 101; © United
States Holocaust Memorial Museum, Washington, D.C., p. 79; Embassy of Israel, p. 83; Enslow Publishers,
Inc., p. 5; Library of Congress, p. 73; MyReportLinks.com Books, p. 4; National Archives, p. 77; United
Nations Cyberschoolbus, p. 18; University of Texas Libraries, p. 16; WNET New York, p. 28.

Cover Photo: AP/Wide World Photos

Cover Description: An Israeli border policeman stands guard as Palestinians exit Jerusalem's Old City
through the Damascus Gate.

Contents

Palestinian Muslims

Orthodox Jews

MyReportLinks.com Books
Great Books, Great Links, Great for Research!

The Internet sites featured in this book can save you hours of research time. These Internet sites—we call them **"Report Links"**—are constantly changing, but we keep them up to date on our Web site.

When you see this "Approved Web Site" logo, you will know that we are directing you to a great Internet site that will help you with your research.

Give it a try! Type http://www.myreportlinks.com into your browser, click on the series title and enter the password, then click on the book title, and scroll down to the Report Links listed for this book.

The Report Links will bring you to great source documents, photographs, and illustrations. MyReportLinks.com Books save you time, feature Report Links that are kept up to date, and make report writing easier than ever! A complete listing of the Report Links can be found on pages 116–117 at the back of the book.

Please see "To Our Readers" on the copyright page for important information about this book, the MyReportLinks.com Web site, and the Report Links that back up this book.

Please enter **NIS1402** if asked for a password.

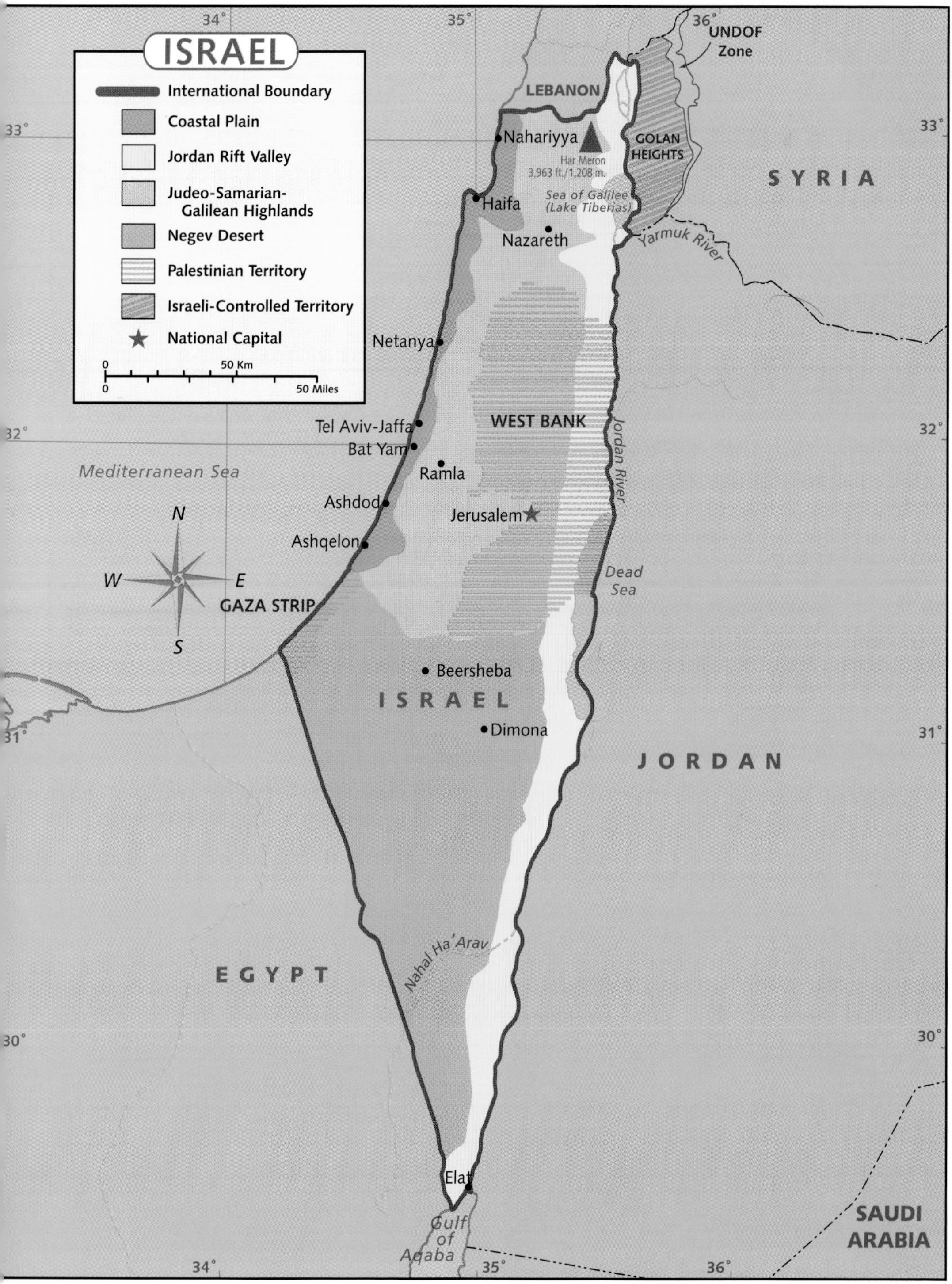

ISRAEL
International Boundary
Coastal Plain
Jordan Rift Valley
Judeo-Samarian-Galilean Highlands
Negev Desert
Palestinian Territory
Israeli-Controlled Territory
National Capital
0
50 Km
0
50 Miles
34°
35°
36°
33°
32°
31°
30°
UNDOF Zone
LEBANON
Nahariyya
Har Meron
3,963 ft./1,208 m.
GOLAN HEIGHTS
SYRIA
Haifa
Sea of Galilee (Lake Tiberias)
Nazareth
Yarmuk River
Netanya
Tel Aviv-Jaffa
WEST BANK
Bat Yam
Jordan River
Mediterranean Sea
Ramla
Ashdod
Jerusalem
N
Ashqelon
W
E
Dead Sea
GAZA STRIP
S
Beersheba
ISRAEL
Dimona
JORDAN
EGYPT
Nahal Ha'Arav
Elat
Gulf of Aqaba
SAUDI ARABIA

Map of Israel

▷ **Flag**
White with a blue hexagram (six-pointed linear star) known as the shield or Star of David; the hexagram is centered between two blue, horizontal bands near the top and bottom edges of the flag

▷ **Official Name**
State of Israel

▷ **Capital**
Jerusalem (though not recognized as such by the United Nations—most nations keep their embassies in Tel Aviv)

▷ **Population**
6.3 million (2005 estimate)

▷ **Area**
20,770 square kilometers

▷ **Highest Point**
Mount Meron at 1,208 meters

▷ **Lowest Point**
Dead Sea at 412 meters below sea level

▷ **Location**
Bordered on the north by Lebanon, to the northeast by Syria, to the east by Jordan, to the southwest by Egypt, and to the west by the Mediterranean Sea

▷ **Type of Government**
parliamentary democracy

▷ **Head of State**
President Moshe Katzav

▷ **Head of Government**
Prime Minister Ehud Olmert (acting)

▷ **Monetary Unit**
Israeli shekel

▷ **Official Language**
Hebrew (and Arabic for the Arab minority)

▷ **National Anthem**
"HaTikvah" ("The Hope")

▷ **National Emblem**
Gold menorah, decorated with olive branches on both sides

▷ **Nationality**
Israeli

▷ **Religion**
Jewish (80 percent) and Muslim (14 percent)

▷ **National Holiday**
Independence Day (May 14)

▷ **Literacy Rate**
95 percent

Old Jerusalem's Jewish Quarter

Time Line

1700 B.C.—Joseph leads Hebrews out of Canaan and into Egypt.

1300 B.C.—Moses leads Hebrews back to Canaan.

586 B.C. —Babylonians conquer Judah. Jews are forced to leave.

539 B.C. —Persians conquer Babylon and Jews are allowed to return.

142 B.C. —Judah becomes independent of Syria.

63 B.C. —Roman Empire takes over Jewish homeland.

A.D. 1290—Jews expelled from England.

1306 —Jews expelled from France.

1492 —Jews expelled from Spain.

1909 —Russian Jews settle first kibbutz along the Sea of Galilee.

**1930s–
1940s** —Germans exterminate an estimated 6 million Jews in what is known as the Holocaust.

1948 —Israel becomes an independent country.

—Israel is attacked by Egypt, Syria, Lebanon, Iraq, and Jordan to start the first Arab-Israeli War.

1956 —Egypt takes control of the Suez Canal, and Israel attacks Egypt with help from France. This is the beginning of the second Arab-Israeli War.

1967 —Israel defeats Egypt, Jordan, and Syria in what is known as the Six-Day War. As a result of the war, Israel captured the Sinai Peninsula, West Bank, Gaza Strip, and the Golan Heights.

1972 —Palestinian terrorists murder seven Israeli athletes at the Summer Olympics held in Munich.

1973 —Israel is attacked by Egypt and Syria. This is called the Yom Kippur War.

1978 —Egypt and Israel sign the Camp David Accords after peace talks are held in the United States. Israel returns to Egypt the portion of the Sinai Peninsula that it still occupied. Agreement is officially signed in 1979.

1982 —Israeli forces led by Ariel Sharon invade Lebanon in an attempt to push the Palestine Liberation Organization (PLO) away from the border.

1987 —Palestinians living in Israel and the occupied areas begin an Intifada.

1993 —Israel and the PLO sign an agreement to attempt to settle their differences.

2000 —Second Intifada begins.

2004 —*November 11:* Palestinian leader Yasser Arafat dies.

2005 —*January:* Mahmoud Abbas is elected leader of the Palestinian Authority.

—*August 15:* Israel begins withdrawal from entire Gaza Strip.

Chapter 1

Another Chance for Peace

While Yasser Arafat lay in a coma in November 2004, the future of Israel and the Palestinians lay in the balance. Arafat was the longtime leader of the Palestinians; Arabs who had been displaced from their homeland since the formation of the Jewish nation of Israel in 1948. Their homeland was Palestine, which included sections of Israel, and the disputed territories of the West Bank and the Gaza Strip. For decades, various leaders had worked to end the land disputes and warfare between Israel and Palestinians. But in recent years, Arafat would not compromise during negotiations. Allegedly, he even contributed to terrorist attacks against Israel. He was, many believed, a roadblock to peace.

At 3:30 A.M. on November 11, Arafat was pronounced dead. While Palestinians and some Israelis mourned, they also prayed that peace was on the horizon.

"The recent events could be a historic turning point for the Middle East," said Israeli Prime Minister Ariel Sharon. "Israel is a country that seeks peace and will continue in its efforts to reach a peace deal with the Palestinians without delay."

However, Sharon added, "I hope that the new Palestinian leadership . . . will understand that the advancement of the relations . . . depends first and foremost on them stopping terror."[1]

True peace between the longtime rivals remained a monumental challenge. Sharon pledged to withdraw from territories that Israel occupied in the West Bank and Gaza Strip, allowing the Palestinian Authority (PA) to take over the land. In a hopeful sign, Palestinians elected Mahmoud Abbas as PA president in January 2005. Far more moderate than Arafat, Abbas offered what he termed "the hand of peace" to Israel.[2]

Yasser Arafat died in a Paris hospital on November 11, 2004. His passing devastated many Palestinians, including twenty-two-year-old Ihab Joaan. The BBC's **In Depth: Death of Arafat** Web site looks at Arafat's legacy and the possibilities for peace between Israel and Palestine.

Unfortunately, Abbas did not speak for all of his people. Islamic terrorist groups, most notably Hamas, denounced negotiations with Israel. Hamas' stated goal was to conquer Israel, the West Bank, and the Gaza Strip—all the land that Palestinian Arabs inhabited prior to the formation of Israel. Hamas and other Islamic extremist groups have employed terror as the means to achieve their goal.

From 2000 to 2006, Hamas suicide bombers killed hundreds of Israeli civilians and put all of the citizenry on edge in what has been called the Al-Aksa Intifada. "The bombings and violence of the last few years have traumatized the population," wrote Donya Meijer of Jerusalem. "Almost everyone knows a family that has suffered the death or maiming of a family member due to terror attacks."[3]

Sharon made it clear that Israel would not make any concessions to the PA until the militant groups refrained from acts of terror. In February 2005, Abbas convinced the major Palestinian extremist groups to agree to a cease-fire. For months the militants complied, and the level of violence diminished greatly. In turn, Israel planned to evacuate all twenty-one Jewish settlements from Gaza in August as well as four of its 120 settlements in the West Bank.

Israel made good on its promise. On August 15, Israeli troops began to evacuate the Gaza settlements as well as the four in the West Bank. Hundreds of Jews, gathered at synagogues, refused to go peacefully. They locked arms to form human chains, making it almost impossible for Israeli riot police to remove them. Nevertheless, all of the targeted settlements were evacuated by August 24.

Predictably, problems persisted in Gaza over the following weeks. In September, Hamas fired rockets from Gaza into Israel, and the Israelis retaliated with air strikes. In October, Iranian President Mahmoud Ahmadinejad added to the tension when he declared that Israel should be "wiped out from the map."

Through it all, Ariel Sharon remained firmly committed to the peace process. In November, he announced he was forming a "new national liberal"

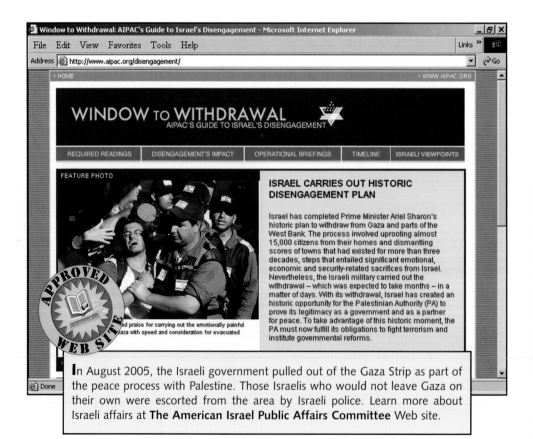

In August 2005, the Israeli government pulled out of the Gaza Strip as part of the peace process with Palestine. Those Israelis who would not leave Gaza on their own were escorted from the area by Israeli police. Learn more about Israeli affairs at **The American Israel Public Affairs Committee** Web site.

▲ *Muslim head coverings for sale at a shop in Israel. Many Israelis are hoping that the withdrawal from the Gaza Strip will lead to peace between themselves and the Palestinians.*

political party and that he aimed to "lay the foundations for a peace settlement." Sharon, however, suffered a massive stroke on January 4, 2006, creating a void of leadership in Israel.

Later in the month, Israelis experienced more unsettling news: Hamas won a majority of seats in Palestine's parliamentary elections. While the peace-seeking Abbas remained president, the terror-based Hamas was now more powerful than ever. Once again, Israeli citizens became pessimistic about achieving true peace, a goal the nation has never achieved.

Chapter 2

Land and Climate

Israel, wrote Rabbi Harold Schulweis, bears "the concerns of a universe," yet "is the size of a postage stamp."[1] Israel is indeed a small country, slightly smaller than the state of New Jersey.

The nation is located in southwest Asia, on the eastern shore of the Mediterranean Sea. Surrounded by Arab nations, Israel's location has contributed to its turmoil. Israel is bordered on the north by Lebanon, on the northeast by Syria, on the east by Jordan, and on the southwest by Egypt. Its southern tip extends to the Gulf of Aqaba, an extension of the Red Sea.

The total area of Israel is about eight thousand square miles. It stretches 260 miles from north to south and between 10 to 70 miles east to west. This total square mileage does not include areas occupied by Israel: the West Bank (2,263 square miles), Golan Heights (1,250 square miles), and East Jerusalem (70 square miles). Though a small nation, Israel has it all geographically: a coastal plain, mountains, valleys, and desert.

▷ Geographical Regions

In all, Israel has four distinct geographical regions. One of them, the coastal plain, runs along the Mediterranean Sea. From east to west, it stretches up to 30 miles. The coastal plain boasts beautiful white-sand beaches as well as fertile farmland. Most Israelis live in this region, which is home to both Tel Aviv and Haifa.

The Galilean-Samarian-Judean Highlands is the region just east of the coastal plain. The highlands are hills that run from Galilee in the north to the Judean Hills in the middle of Israel. The Galilean Highlands are dominated by hills and valleys. Mount Meron (3,963 feet) is the highest point in

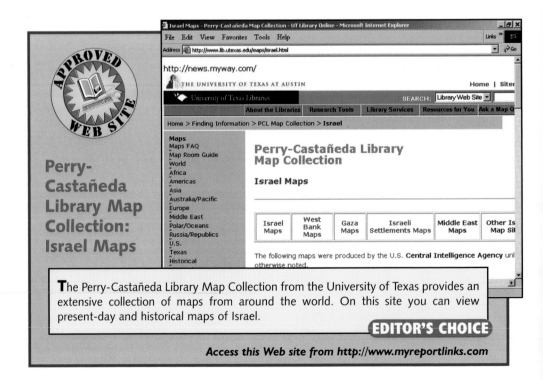

Perry-Castañeda Library Map Collection: Israel Maps

The Perry-Castañeda Library Map Collection from the University of Texas provides an extensive collection of maps from around the world. On this site you can view present-day and historical maps of Israel.

EDITOR'S CHOICE

Access this Web site from http://www.myreportlinks.com

Israel. In the valleys, villagers cultivate orchards and vineyards. The Samarian Hills, a mountainous area, comprise the central portion of the region. The Judean Hills, located in the southern part of the region, are steep and rocky. They are the setting for the city of Jerusalem, which sits 2,500 feet above sea level.

The Jordan Rift Valley runs along Israel's eastern border. The region is actually part of a geographical trench called the Great Rift Valley, which extends from Syria to southern Africa. The Jordan River and the Sea of Galilee are located in the northern section of the Jordan Rift Valley. The southern portion of the valley dips well below sea level. Except for the Dead Sea, the land there is hard and dry.

The Negev Desert comprises the southernmost region of Israel. It extends from the city of Beersheba in the north to the Gulf of Aqaba in the south. Except for a low mountain chain along the north of the region, the desert is flat with hardpan gravel. The town of Elat, at the northern edge of the region along the Red Sea, attracts many tourists.

▶ Bodies of Water

Israel is home to some of the most famous bodies of water in the world. The Jordan River runs along Israel's eastern border. It begins at the base of Mount Hermon in the Golan Heights and flows south to the Dead Sea. Though narrow and shallow, the Jordan

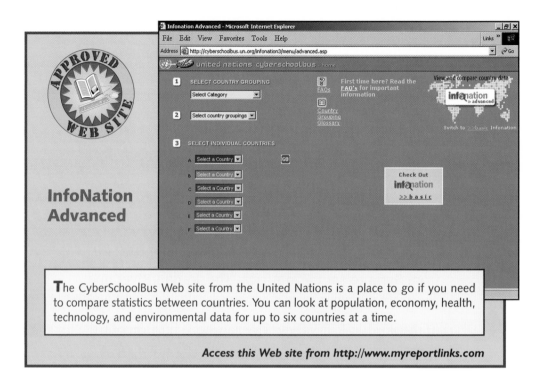

InfoNation Advanced

The CyberSchoolBus Web site from the United Nations is a place to go if you need to compare statistics between countries. You can look at population, economy, health, technology, and environmental data for up to six countries at a time.

Access this Web site from http://www.myreportlinks.com

River is an extremely important source of water for Israel, Jordan, Syria, Lebanon, and the Palestinians.

The Sea of Galilee, also known as Lake Tiberias, is tucked into the northeast corner of Israel. This, according to Scripture, is where Jesus was baptized. A freshwater sea, it attracts many vacationers, including boaters and campers.

The Dead Sea got its name because fish and vegetation cannot live in it. It is just too salty—much more so than ocean water. Though not recommended for swimming, some people like to float on the sea (the salty water makes them buoyant). The Dead Sea, which is rich with minerals, happens to be the lowest place on earth. It is more than 1,300 feet below sea level.

Natural Resources

Israel is not blessed with great resources. Unlike its Arab neighbors, it contains very little oil and natural gas. Moreover, less than 20 percent of Israel's land is suitable for agriculture. In fact, farming on much of the land would be impossible if it were not for Israel's sophisticated irrigation systems. Only the coastal plain, the interior valleys, and the northern Negev contain fertile soil. Fortunately, certain areas of Israel are rich in minerals, especially the Dead Sea and the Negev.

Climate

Despite the small size of the country, temperatures vary significantly in Israel. It depends on three things: location, elevation, and exposure to the sea. In the coastal plains, including Haifa and Tel Aviv, average daytime highs range from 62°F in the winter to 88°F in the summer. In upland regions such as Jerusalem, average temps vary from 51°F in the winter to 82°F in the summer. In the desert, summer temperatures can exceed 100°F.

Except in the hills and mountains, snow rarely falls in Israel. Winters tend to be chilly with lots of rain. After many months of warm, dry weather, many Israelis welcome the change. "The best part of Israeli weather, I'd say, would be the morning after a

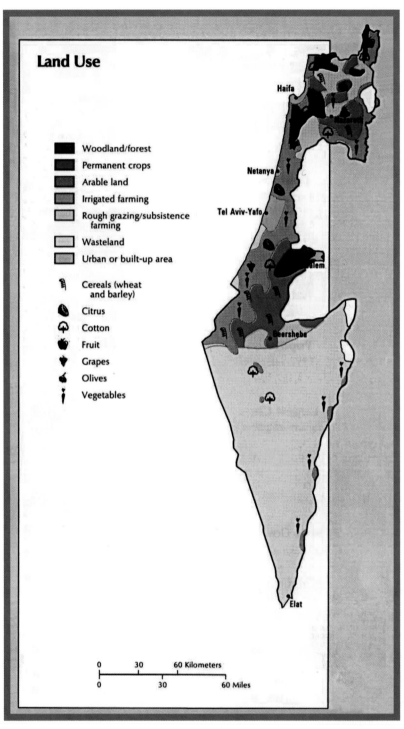

Land Use

Legend:
- Woodland/forest
- Permanent crops
- Arable land
- Irrigated farming
- Rough grazing/subsistence farming
- Wasteland
- Urban or built-up area

- Cereals (wheat and barley)
- Citrus
- Cotton
- Fruit
- Grapes
- Olives
- Vegetables

Haifa

Nazareth

Netanya

Tel Aviv-Yafo

Jerusalem

Beersheba

Elat

0   30   60 Kilometers

0   30   60 Miles

▲ This map shows what type of terrain can be found in each part of Israel, as well as some of the major crops grown in each area.

winter night, when the smell of rain is in the air," wrote Meir Brooks, a resident of Haifa. "The air is cold but not freezing, and very, very damp. It has a good feeling to it."[2]

Conversely, added Meir Fishburn of Kfar Saba, Israel, "the worst weather is definitely the Sharav— hot, dry, dust-laden winds which we suffer at the change of season in the autumn and spring. Temperatures go right up to the hundreds."[3]

Plant and Animal Life

All told, Israel boasts about twenty-five hundred species of plants. Although it does not rain much during the warm months, most of these species can endure long dry spells. Wildflowers, common in

Israel Ministry of Foreign Affairs: Photo Exhibits

On the Israel Ministry of Foreign Affairs Web site, you will find a collection of photo exhibits from various places in Israel.

Access this Web site from http://www.myreportlinks.com

Israel, bring color and cheer to the citizenry. Because of centuries of cultivation and herding, Israel's evergreen forests largely disappeared. However, through a reforestation program, large numbers of trees have been planted, especially in the hilly regions.

Israel boasts about a hundred species of mammals. Such fascinating animals as wild boars, gazelles, hyenas, ibexes, jackals, and wildcats roam the land. Farmers raise chickens, sheep, and cows. Moreover, Israel is a bird-watcher's dream come true. It is home to up to five hundred varieties of birds—more than any other country of comparable

▲ *A Muslim girl rides a jackal along a road by Jerusalem.*

The Environment in Israel - Microsoft Internet Explorer

JEWISH VIRTUAL LIBRARY
A Division of The American-Israeli Cooperative Enterprise

The Environment in Israel

By D'vora Ben-Shaul

Ask any environmentally aware and informed person what are Israel's critically important environmental issues and they will no doubt all come up with more or less the same list. But if you ask them to arrange the issues in order of priority you will probably get as many opinions as you have participants. This is not unexpected because not only is Israel's list of environmental problems large, but there are so many factors to be considered that priorities are, to a great extent, in the eye of the beholder and depend on the particular area with which they are in personal contact. Therefore I have listed the topics here alphabetically and not according to any particular priority; they are simply the issues at stake.

Jewish Virtual Library: The Environment in Israel

Israel faces many major environmental concerns. Learn more about these issues and what is being done to help fix these problems.

Access this Web site from http://www.myreportlinks.com

size. Such birds as partridge, bustard, sand grouse, cuckoo, and desert lark fly the Israeli skies.

Farmers in southern parts of Israel worry about swarms of locusts invading from Africa. These large insects severely damaged crops in November 2004. "If these pests land on my fields, it's all over," said potato farmer Menachem Tzafrir. "They destroy a whole year's work in a matter of minutes."[4]

▶ Environmental Concerns

As a crowded, urbanized country, Israel faces serious environmental issues. Factories and a large number of cars pollute the air, while untreated sewage contaminates waterways.

As for air pollution, "The Haifa area tends to suffer more," wrote Fishburn. "At certain times of the year, Tel Aviv suffers from traffic exhaust pollution, especially when there is little or no wind to blow it away." He added that "there is a severe and increasing pollution problem . . . produced by the Palestinian Authority areas, who do not attempt to control their sewage."[5]

Israeli officials have taken steps to deal with these problems. They have required catalytic converters for cars, and they have eliminated leaded gasoline. Much has been done to clean polluted water. For example, fish had all but disappeared in the Yarkon River, but they have come back since a clean-up campaign was instituted. The raw sewage problem remains a serious issue.

For Israelis, their homeland is dear to them, and they are determined to keep it clean. "There is a 'green' movement here," wrote Naomi Leitner of Kfar Saba, Israel, "and people do protest ecological degradation."[6]

The Jewish Faith

According to the Bible's Book of Genesis, about four thousand years ago, God spoke to Abraham, the leader of a seminomadic people living in what was then Mesopotamia. God told Abraham to lead his followers to Canaan (now Israel and Lebanon), and He made a covenant (agreement) with Abraham: If Abraham agreed to obey Him, God would protect Abraham's people in their new home. Thus, Abraham led his followers to Canaan . . . and the history of the world was altered forever.

The modern State of Israel was founded in 1948 with Judaism as its official religion. Those who adhere to Judaism are called Jews, and Jews trace their history back to Abraham's covenant with God. The Jewish faith is based on the Torah (the five books of Moses, which are the first five books of the Bible) and the remainder of the Bible's Old Testament. Many of the historical details have been disputed by scholars, while other facts have been confirmed by archaeologists. Nonetheless, Orthodox Jews (those Jews who adhere to a strict interpretation of Jewish law and customs) believe that they

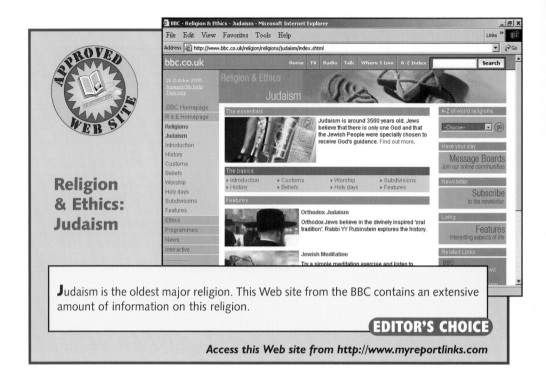

Religion & Ethics: Judaism

Judaism is the oldest major religion. This Web site from the BBC contains an extensive amount of information on this religion.

EDITOR'S CHOICE

Access this Web site from http://www.myreportlinks.com

have a covenant with God and that the story that follows is true.

Joseph and Moses

Abraham's people lived peacefully in Canaan and became known as Hebrews. However, due to a famine and drought around 1700 B.C., Abraham's great-grandson Joseph led the Hebrews out of Canaan to Egypt. A few years later, the Egyptian pharaoh forced the Hebrews into slavery, where they remained for nearly four hundred years. Around 1300 B.C., Moses was living in a land called Midian when God inspired him to go to Egypt and lead the Hebrews back to Canaan.

During their forty-year journey to Canaan, Moses and the Hebrews promised to worship only God. God rewarded their loyalty by making the Hebrews his "chosen people" and guaranteeing that Canaan would flow with "milk and honey." God also gave Moses the Ten Commandments, rules for his people to live by.

Now calling themselves the Israelites, Moses and his followers made it to Canaan. The land, however, flowed not with milk and honey but with human blood. Unwelcoming, the Canaanites fought the Israelites for many years, finally succumbing in the eleventh century when Joshua, one of Moses' lieutenants, led the Israelites to victory. But more trouble followed. The Philistines arrived in Canaan, and they were armed and hostile. To best defend themselves, the twelve Israelite tribes banded together and chose a king, Saul, in 1020 B.C.

▷ Three Great Kings

Saul led his people to success against the Philistines, but he was killed in battle in 1000 B.C. A great warrior named David was proclaimed king, and he led the Israelites to ultimate victory over the Philistines. David unified the twelve tribes into one nation, the kingdom of Israel, with a shared faith. Upon his death in 961 B.C., his son, Solomon, became king.

Solomon strengthened the kingdom. He built a lavish royal palace and a great temple in

Heritage: Civilization and the Jews is a very informative series and Web site from PBS. Important historical events in Jewish history are covered. Each time period from 3800 B.C. to the 1990s includes interactive portions and historical documents.

Access this Web site from http://www.myreportlinks.com

Jerusalem, Canaan's capital city. Called the First Temple, it took seventy thousand men more than seven years to build. Many Hebrews resented the labor and taxes required to construct Solomon's buildings. Solomon's heir—his son, Rehoboam— was even harsher. In rebellion, ten of Canaan's tribes formed their own nation in the northern part of the Israeli kingdom. Rehoboam remained as ruler of the southern kingdom, which became known as Judah.

In the 700s B.C., Assyrians invaded an unstable Israel and took over the land. The fate of the ten "lost tribes" is unknown. In 586 B.C., the

Babylonians took over Judah, burning Jerusalem and destroying the great First Temple. The people of Judah, known as the Jews, were sent to Babylonia. Only in 539 B.C., when Persia conquered Babylonia, were the Jews allowed to return to Judah. Forty thousand Jews did, and they constructed the Second Temple in Jerusalem.

Although these Jews lived in their homeland, Persia controlled the region. The area was conquered by Alexander the Great of Macedonia followed by the Ptolemies of Egypt and then Antiochus IV of Syria. In 142 B.C., the Jews successfully rebelled against the oppressive Antiochus, and Judah became independent. For a few decades, the Jews had their own state—until the mighty Roman Empire took control of the region in 63 B.C. For the next two thousand years, Jews would remain stateless.

▷ Roman Rule

For three hundred years, the Romans ruled Judah, an area which they called Palestine. It was a Roman governor, Pontius Pilate, who sentenced Jesus Christ, a Jew, to death. While many in the region (the first Christians) would come to regard Jesus as the son of God, Jews did not hold this belief.

Jews became unhappy with Roman rule. In A.D. 66, the Zealots—Jews who demanded independence—rebelled against Roman legions. In A.D. 70, Titus led a Roman reprisal. The Romans destroyed Jerusalem and the Second Temple,

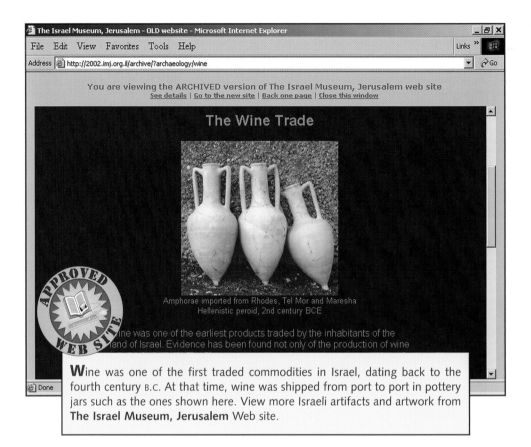

The Israel Museum, Jerusalem - OLD website - Microsoft Internet Explorer

File   Edit   View   Favorites   Tools   Help   Links »

Address http://2002.imj.org.il/archive/?archaeology/wine   Go

You are viewing the ARCHIVED version of The Israel Museum, Jerusalem web site
See details | Go to the new site | Back one page | Close this window

The Wine Trade

Amphorae imported from Rhodes, Tel Mor and Maresha
Hellenistic peroid, 2nd century BCE

ine was one of the earliest products traded by the inhabitants of the
and of Israel. Evidence has been found not only of the production of wine

Wine was one of the first traded commodities in Israel, dating back to the fourth century B.C. At that time, wine was shipped from port to port in pottery jars such as the ones shown here. View more Israeli artifacts and artwork from **The Israel Museum, Jerusalem** Web site.

leaving only one wall (known as the Wailing Wall) remaining. According to Jewish faith, this is the state in which the temple is to remain until a descendant of David arises to restore the glory of Israel.

▶ Jewish Principles of Faith

Four thousand years ago, Judaism was unique for its time because it was a monotheistic religion. While their contemporaries worshiped multiple gods, Hebrews believed in just one god. In all, there are thirteen principles of Jewish faith:

I. God is one. God created the universe and is the source of morality. Unlike Christians, Jews do not believe in a holy trinity (God, Christ, and the Holy Spirit).

II. God is omnipotent (all powerful) and omniscient (all knowing).

III. God does not have a physical form, and God is eternal.

IV. Jews may pray only to God.

V. The Hebrew Bible is the product of divine revelation.

VI. The words of the prophets are true.

VII. Moses was the chief of all prophets.

VIII. The Torah is the primary text of Judaism.

IX. God will reward those who observe His commandments, and He will punish those who violate them.

X. Jews are God's chosen people.

XI. A Messiah (savior) will one day come to earth.

XII. The soul is pure at birth. People have free will, meaning they can make their own choices.

XIII. People can atone (make up) for their sins through their words and deeds.

Over the last two centuries, different Jewish denominations have emerged. Although each adheres to the basic principles of Judaism, their theologies differ. Orthodox Jews believe that the Torah was written by God and dictated to Moses, and that the laws are binding. Other denominations

The Torah - Microsoft Internet Explorer

File　Edit　View　Favorites　Tools　Help

Address http://www.wsu.edu:8080/~dee/HEBREWS/TORAH.HTM

The Torah

The Torah

The foundation of Hebrew and Jewish religion, thought, law, and society is the **Torah**. The Torah, consisting of five books, lays down the central events of Hebrew history: the beginning of time, the election of Abraham, the history of the patriarchs, and the monumental history of the deliverance of the Hebrews from Egypt under the leadership of Moses. The Torah overwhelmingly concerns this last historical event, the event that gave the Hebrews a religion, a nation, and an identity: the "bene yisrael," the "children of Israel." The migration from Egypt involved two crucial events: the introduction to Yahweh on Mount Sinai and the receiving of Yahweh's religious and social instructions.

Torah is typically translated "**law**," but it also means something like "instructions" or "directions." For these five books are Yahweh's rules or directions for life and worship. The bulk of the books consist of cultic rules, but the whole of Hebrew law is contained in these books. Above these laws tower the laws given by Yahweh directly to his people: the Decalogue or ten commandments. This is the only part of the Hebrew scriptures that purports to be the direct speech of Yahweh *written down on the spot*. The decalogue forms the center of all the rules and laws developed out of them.

The salient feature of the Torah as the law of the Hebrews is its divine origins and its immutability. The Torah as law is seen as the instructions given to the chosen people by the one and only one God, Yahweh. The special relationship between the Hebrews and Yahweh is predicated on *obedience* : the Torah itself stands in for Yahweh. In every sense of the word, if

On this Web site, you will learn more about the Torah. The Torah is the foundation of Jewish religion, thought, law, and society.

Access this Web site from http://www.myreportlinks.com

include Conservative Judaism, Reconstructionist Judaism, and Reform Judaism.

In Israel, one's denomination is not as important as his or her commitment to Judaism. Jews are considered observant, or religious, if they keep kosher and observe Jewish holidays and Shabbat (a day of rest and worship that lasts from Friday evening to Saturday evening). Those who do not follow these religious laws are considered nonreligious, or secular.

▶ Religious Versus Secular Jews

Being a religious Jew requires great sacrifice, as adherents must devote much of their lives to God.

Most Israelis simply are not that committed to their religion. Called secular Jews, they comprise about 80 percent of Israel's population. They often clash with their religious countrymen.

Wrote secular Israeli Daphna Baram:

In 1987, young secular Jerusalemites rebelled against the 'Saturday night curfew' that used to be

▲ Devout, Orthodox Jews hurry to worship. Conservative and Orthodox Jews often have very different opinions than the more secular Jews in Israel.

imposed on the city. My generation of high school students genuinely believed . . . that religious coercion was the biggest problem of Israeli society. We rallied outside Jerusalem's closed cinemas every Saturday night, and looked scornfully on our opponents, Orthodox youngsters who walked all the way from their remote neighborhoods to participate in counter-demonstrations.[1]

Today, ultra-Orthodox Jews wish to impose strict religious law on all aspects of Israeli life. They often look down on nonpracticing Jews, who they feel are breaking their covenant with God. Conversely, many secular Jews rebel against the old ways, including strict observance of Shabbat. Moreover, many women object to the fact that they have to pray behind a barrier, apart from the men, at Jerusalem's Western (Wailing) Wall.

Many Israelis resent what they see as special favors for ultra-Orthodox Jews. Some ultra-Orthodox devote their lives to studying the Torah—and are supported by working citizens' tax dollars. Some secular soldiers are angered by the fact that ultra-Orthodox Israelis are exempt from serving in the military.

Religion in Israeli Politics

Religion plays a major role in Israeli politics. The Knesset, the legislative branch of the Israeli government, is comprised of many political parties. Several of these parties have strong religious agendas.

▲ These Muslim girls are chatting at the Damascus Gate Market. Arab Muslims make up about 14 percent of the Israeli population.

The Shas and the United Torah, which are both ultra-Orthodox, are among the religious parties that wield heavy influence in the Knesset.

Despite the country's roots in Judaism, Israeli law guarantees religious freedom. Such tolerance is imperative since about 14 percent of Israelis are Arab Muslims. Muslims believe that Allah (Arabic for God) is the only deity, and that Muhammad was his messenger. Ironically, secular and ultra-Orthodox

Jews clash more over religion with each other than they do with Israeli Muslims.

Interestingly, Israel has only the second largest Jewish population in the world. The nation's 5.2 million Jews are a smaller group than the 5.5 million in the United States. America's Jews share a kinship with Israel. At least partly for this reason, the United States has been a strong ally of Israel. A strong American-Israeli group, the American Israel Public Affairs Committee (AIPAC), lobbies in Washington for the political and economic support of Israel.

Jews as a Persecuted People

Over the the centuries, Jews have paid an enormous price for adherence to their faith. In fact, no religious group in world history has been persecuted so severely.

In the decades and centuries after the crucifixion of Christ, Christians blamed Jews for turning in Jesus to the Roman authorities. Jews came to be depicted as "Christ killers" and guilty of deicide, the murder of the incarnation of God (a belief that today's Vatican has renounced). Over the centuries, some renowned Christian religious experts wrote hate-fully about Jews and Judaism. Martin Luther, the founder of the Lutheran faith, for example, advocated the burning of synagogues and driving Jews "like mad dogs out of the land."[2]

For centuries, Jews were oppressed, demonized, and murdered throughout Europe. Laws banned Jews from marrying Christians, owning land, and participating in certain professions. During the Crusades in the eleventh, twelfth, and thirteenth centuries, thousands of Jews were slaughtered as Christians "purified" their European territory. Ghettos were established for Jews, and Christians increasingly identified Jews with Satan. Jews were expelled from England in 1290, from France in 1306, and from Spain in 1492.

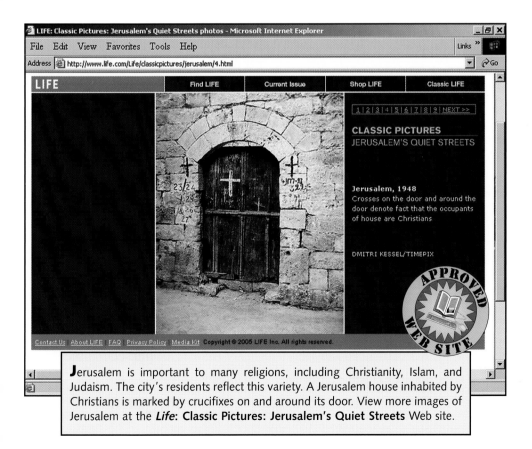

Jerusalem is important to many religions, including Christianity, Islam, and Judaism. The city's residents reflect this variety. A Jerusalem house inhabited by Christians is marked by crucifixes on and around its door. View more images of Jerusalem at the *Life*: **Classic Pictures: Jerusalem's Quiet Streets** Web site.

Often, Christians falsely accused Jews of "blood libel"—killing Christians and drinking their blood. Such a rumor could cause angry Christians to slaughter a whole village of Jews. Religious differences were only one reason for anti-Semitism (which is defined as opposition to and discrimination against Jews). Wrote Holocaust scholar John Roth: "Jews have been discriminated against, hated, and killed because prejudiced non-Jews believed they belonged to the wrong religion, lacked citizenship qualifications, practiced business improperly, behaved inappropriately, or possessed inferior racial characteristics."[3]

Hatred of Jews continued in Europe up through the twentieth century. From 1919 through 1921, Christian Poles and Ukrainians attacked and murdered more than sixty thousand Jews. During the Holocaust in the late 1930s and 1940s, nearly a hundred times that many Jews were exterminated.

"All Israeli Jews are aware of the Holocaust on a very immediate level," wrote Naomi Leitner. "The fear of another annihilation is still very strong. This is what our enemies promise to do to us, and most of us believe they will do it if they can."[4]

▶ Fear of Anti-Semitism Today

According to Leitner, the Jews' history of persecution makes them sympathetic to other oppressed people. "We watch in horror as one group after another is slaughtered and nobody cares," she wrote. "The best

▲ *This Israeli boy is taking part in a Jewish bar mitzvah celebration. This rite of passage takes place on a boy's thirteenth birthday. Jewish girls celebrate a similar rite, called a bat mitzvah.*

we can do is take care of our own—such as airlifting the Ethiopian Jews to Israel—and make the gestures that a small country can make. Israel took in Muslims from Bosnia and always sends medical teams to disaster areas."[5]

For Jews, the history of anti-Semitism is ever present in their thoughts and actions. "Israelis usually feel that they have always been the small, isolated, and persecuted people who have to struggle to succeed," wrote Meir Brooks of Haifa, Israel. "Most Israelis are, as a result, defiant in their nature. They wish to defy expectations; do well when all expect them to fail; fight back when others think they will surrender."[6]

Persecuted since Biblical times, Jews remain firmly committed to their God, their religion, and each other. "We are one people, no matter where we live, constantly fighting for our right to be," wrote Shelley Yachbesh of Moshav Neve Yamin, Israel. "I don't think any group of people has survived like us, and it is because of our faith."[7]

Israeli Culture

No nation in the world even remotely compares to Israel. The nation rests on ancient Holy Land, yet it ranks among the world's most modernized and urbanized countries. It also is the only country that is predominantly Jewish. Most Israelis have family members who were murdered because of their faith during the Holocaust, creating a powerful bond among the citizenry.

Israel is surrounded by Arab nations that have been enemies to the Jewish state. Yet about 14 percent of Israel's 6.3 million citizens are Arabs. Moreover, Israelis share occupied territories with Palestinians, Israel's longtime foes. War and fear have been part of daily Israeli life since the nation's inception. When tensions escalate, like they did in the early 2000s, citizens constantly live on edge.

"There was a period when we had a suicide bombing every day," wrote Naomi Leitner. "We also had tremendous security precautions everywhere— you were frisked and had your bag checked in a very intrusive way all the time.

"We were constantly making insane calculations: How dangerous is it for my son to ride the bus to a

Israel is a country with ancient structures, modern cities, and sandy beaches. Many Israelis like to relax along the beach at the city called Caesarea.

friend's house? Is it reasonable for my daughter to shop at the mall? Will I forgive myself if she goes shopping and something happens? Do we see the movie we really want to see or go to the theater with better security? Do we go out for a pizza or is it safer to order in?"[1]

Because of the political uncertainty, wrote Israeli Shelley Yachbesh, "children as well as adults tend to live in the moment."[2]

▶ Israeli Government

Like the United States, Israel has a president. However, it is largely a figurehead position. The head of government is the prime minister, who had been Ariel Sharon since 2001. Sharon presided over

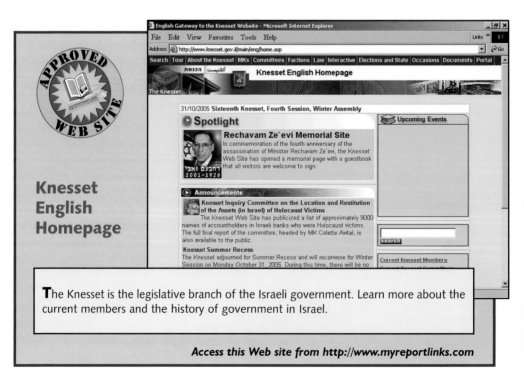

Knesset English Homepage

The Knesset is the legislative branch of the Israeli government. Learn more about the current members and the history of government in Israel.

Access this Web site from http://www.myreportlinks.com

the 120-member Knesset—Israel's parliament until he had a major stroke on January 4, 2006. Ehud Olmert took over as acting prime minister until the elections scheduled for March 28.

Israel has universal suffrage, meaning all adult citizens, male and female, can vote. In national elections for the Knesset, citizens vote for the party of their choice. The more votes a party receives, the more seats it will be allocated in the Knesset. However, there are more than a dozen parties in the Knesset, and typically no party receives more than twenty-some seats. Thus, many different voices and agendas are heard in the Knesset.

The Knesset also elects a prime minister, who typically represents the largest party. However, since even the largest party does not have a majority of seats in the Knesset, the prime minister must build a coalition of parties to further his or her agenda. Thus, even a small party can have its voice heard if it becomes part of the ruling party's coalition.

▷ Political Parties and The Judiciary

In the past thirty years, the largest political parties have been the conservative Likud Party and the social-democrat Labor Party. Other important parties include the ultra-Orthodox Shas (who support social spending) and the Shinui (secularists). The National Union represents the most conservative citizens, while the Yachad supports achieving peace with the Palestinians. Several parties have strong religious agendas.

Israel's judicial system is much like that in the United States. It has a three-tier system of courts, with the Supreme Court at the top, and places a strong emphasis on civil rights. Israel, for example, is the only Middle Eastern country that grants full rights to homosexuals. In addition to civil courts, Israel has religious courts (Jewish, Muslim, and Christian) for such issues as marriage and divorce.

▶ Ethnic Groups

In the early years of the State of Israel, Jews often were classified into two groups. The Ashkenazic Jews hailed from Europe, while the Sephardic Jews came from the Middle East, North Africa, Spain, and the Mediterranean region. The two groups differed in religious rites, pronunciation of Hebrew, and social customs. On the whole, Ashkenazic Jews dominated political life and had better education and jobs.

Animosity once existed between the two groups, but that has diminished over time. "Since their children go to the same schools, live in the same neighborhoods, and join the same youth movements, these differences are gradually disappearing," wrote Donya Meijer of Jerusalem. "Intermarriage between the two are common and completely accepted in most circles."[3]

Prior to Israel's formation in 1948, the region

(then known as Palestine) was comprised of Jews and Arabs. Most Arabs fled Israel over the years, but many stayed. Today, more than a million Arabs are Israeli citizens. These Arabs have full legal rights, but many live in separate areas. Moreover, they attend separate schools, speak a different language, and follow different cultural traditions. Animosity exists between Jews and Arabs, especially whenever the Palestinian-Israeli crisis heats up.

Recalled Jonah Schiffmiller, "Before war started a few years ago, many Jews would go into Arab towns to shop or to eat. But when the war started and Israeli Arabs started rioting, all of that ended."[4] Many Arabs who owned businesses, such as auto

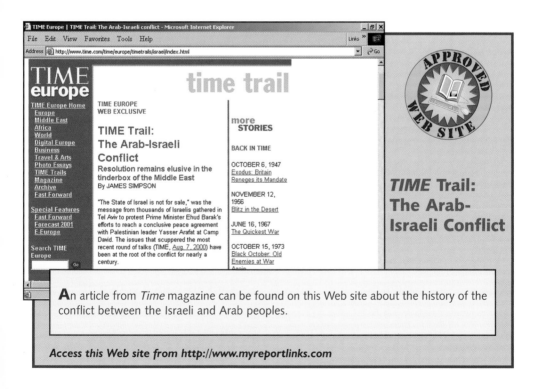

An article from *Time* magazine can be found on this Web site about the history of the conflict between the Israeli and Arab peoples.

Access this Web site from http://www.myreportlinks.com

shops or restaurants, have been hurt by a drop in Israeli patronage.

Shelley Yachbesh adds that Arabs "still feel they are second-class citizens. Okay maybe so, but their track record of helping terrorists makes them untrustworthy."[5] Meir Brooks of Haifa recognizes that racism exists among Israeli Jews toward their country's Arabs. "I have heard many times of acts committed against Israeli Arabs and of terrible slogans and chants against them," Brooks wrote. "Thankfully, however, the government endorses none of this, and legally the status of Arab Israelis is fine."[6]

As long as the disagreements with the Palestinian people are unsettled, discord between Israeli Jews and Arabs undoubtedly will continue.

▶ Language

After the Zionist movement began in the 1890s, Jews from all over the world migrated to Palestine, or what they called Eretz Israel. These Jews shared a common faith, but they did not share a common language. Planners knew that if Eretz Israel was to survive as a Jewish homeland, everyone needed to communicate. Following the lead of Eliezer Ben Yehuda, Hebrew became the official language of Eretz Israel.

Hebrew had not been spoken since ancient times, dying out around 250 B.C., but it had survived in the Torah and other texts. In 1890, Ben Yehuda cofounded the Committee of the Hebrew Language,

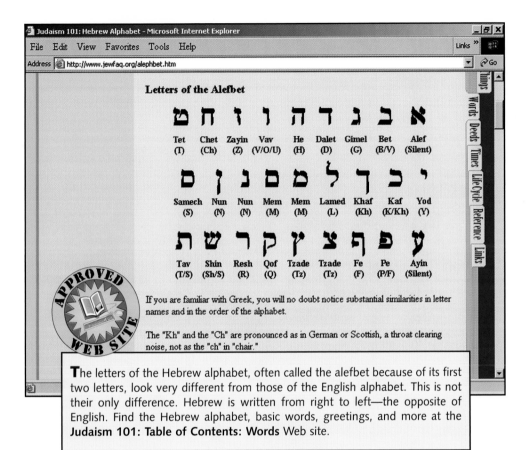

The letters of the Hebrew alphabet, often called the alefbet because of its first two letters, look very different from those of the English alphabet. This is not their only difference. Hebrew is written from right to left—the opposite of English. Find the Hebrew alphabet, basic words, greetings, and more at the **Judaism 101: Table of Contents: Words** Web site.

which is now known as the Academy of the Hebrew Language. Scholars and linguists added new words to the Hebrew language for things that had not existed more than two thousand years earlier. When Israel was founded in 1948, Hebrew was named the official language along with Arabic. Growing children and most immigrants are taught the once ancient, but once again modern language of Hebrew.

Israelis speak other languages as well. Arab Israelis speak Arabic in their communities, and many

The city of Tel Aviv is Israel's major metropolitan center.

Israelis learn English as a second or third language. Of course, recent immigrants to Israel speak their native language in their homes. Some immigrant Jews from Eastern Europe still speak Yiddish, which in Yiddish means "Jewish." That language is slowly dying out, spoken by only about 3 million people worldwide. It is being replaced by Hebrew in Israel, and by local languages elsewhere. Many Jews find the sound of certain Yiddish words amusing. *Shlemil* and *shmendrik,* for example, both mean "fool," while *mishmash* means "hodgepodge."

▶ City Life

"One feels," wrote Donya Meijer, "that Jerusalem is the center of the world."[7] With a population of 680,000, Jerusalem is a bustling city steeped in history. The section of Jerusalem called the "Old City" is surrounded by walls and is comprised of four quarters: Jewish, Muslim, Christian, and Armenian. The Old City is home to the Western (Wailing) Wall, the only remains of the Second Temple, as well as the Dome of the Rock, where it is said that Muhammad ascended to Heaven. Moreover, Christians believe that Jesus performed his Last Supper in Jerusalem and was crucified nearby.

Since Israel's victory in the Six-Day War in 1967, the nation has controlled the entire city of Jerusalem. Israel claims Jerusalem as its capital, although no other countries recognize it as such.

Palestinians, in fact, claim that Jerusalem should be the capital of a future Palestinian state.

As it is, the city is strikingly diverse, offering everything from vegetable markets to modern office buildings to first-class hotels. "Jerusalem is the most beautiful and exciting city in the world, in my eyes," wrote Meijer. "We have the seat of government here, and like Washington, we now have a new Holocaust Memorial Museum. The Supreme Court, museums, theatre, and concert halls are on a par with any."[8]

▶ Tel Aviv

With 350,000 people, Tel Aviv is Israel's second largest city, and the Tel Aviv-Jaffa metropolitan area is home to more than a million people. A Westernized city, Tel Aviv is where the action is: restaurants, nightlife, opera, ballet, museums, sporting events, and much more. Getting full use out of the Mediterranean Sea, boaters and sunbathers enjoy Tel Aviv's marina and beaches. Wealthy Israelis, as well as tourists, shop in the fashionable stores of Tel Aviv's Dizengoff Square. In addition, most foreign countries maintain their embassies in Tel Aviv. Jaffa is more of an old-world city, now famous for its plethora of art galleries.

▶ Haifa

Haifa, with close to three hundred thousand people, is Israel's third most populous city. Resting along the Mediterranean coast, with a spectacular bay,

▲ *This woman is teaching students on an Israeli kibbutz.*

Haifa boasts one of the largest ports in Israel. The city is home to a major oil refinery and many high-tech companies. Beersheba is the largest city of the Negev Desert. It is said that Abraham dug Beersheba's water well about four thousand years ago. Modern technology now provides water to about two hundred thousand Beersheba citizens.

▷ **Kibbutzim and Moshavim**

In 1909 a group of Russian Jews settled near the Sea of Galilee with a set of ideals. They wanted to create a farming community in which land, food, and resources were equally shared. Nearly a century later, their legacy remains in the kibbutzim (plural for kibbutz). Thousands of Israelis live on kibbutzim. Residents own all property collectively, and they contribute work in exchange for basic necessities. Though farming remains the staple of kibbutzim, others make products such as shoes or toys. All eat together at a common table. Many Israelis love the community spirit and simplicity of the kibbutzim lifestyle.

A moshav is similar to a kibbutz, although each family has more independence. Although moshav families purchase and sell goods cooperatively, each family owns its own farmland and lives in its own home. Both the kibbutz and moshav are unique to Israel and are wonderful examples of people working and sharing together.

Emphasis on Education

Traditionally, education has been exceptionally important to Jews and Israelis. Wrote Naomi Leitner: "Israelis like to think of themselves as the People of the Book, and I mean not only the Bible, but in general—a nation of education and readers."[9] Their commitment to education is reflected in the nation's literacy rate, which is 95 percent.

For Israeli kids, school starts early in life. Most children begin kindergarten at age three. From age five to sixteen, school is compulsory. According to

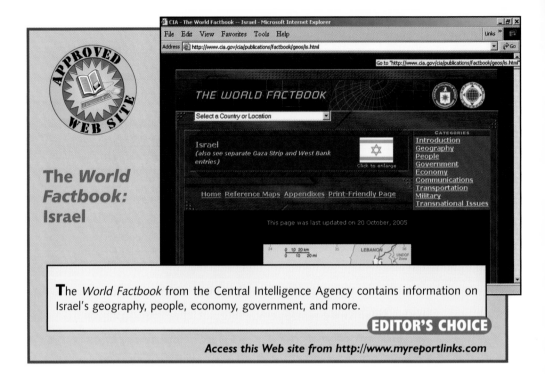

The *World Factbook* from the Central Intelligence Agency contains information on Israel's geography, people, economy, government, and more.

EDITOR'S CHOICE

Access this Web site from http://www.myreportlinks.com

Burton Ravins of Jerusalem, students have "parental support all the way—from preschool classes through university."[10]

Jewish children attend either state-run secular schools or religious schools, all of which teach the national language of Hebrew. Arab children attend separate schools. Their instruction is in Arabic, and their teachers emphasize their people's history, religion, and culture.

Most children go to a secondary school, which is like an American high school. There, they may take university preparatory courses or vocational or trade classes. Some secondary schools specialize in agricultural, technological, military, or religious studies.

Israeli education boasts exceptional universities and vocational schools. "We have internationally recognized universities," wrote Meir Fishburn, "including the Technion in Haifa for advanced scientific studies and the Bezalel School of Art at Jerusalem. Last but not least, there are many, many Yeshivot—Jewish religious seminaries."[11]

▷ Military Service and Education

Before pursuing higher education, however, most students complete compulsory military service. (Exceptions include ultra-Orthodox Jews and Arab Israelis.) Young men must serve three years and women two. Only men are assigned to combat duty. As part of their service, the men and women learn about the Holocaust so that they know why Jewish people need to defend themselves. After serving in the military, Israelis become part of the national reserves. If needed, they will be prepared to fight.

Adult education is also important in Israel due to the high number of adult immigrants. Those Jews who arrive from foreign lands need to learn Hebrew and prepare for new jobs.

Though education is highly valued in Israel, some parents in recent years were afraid to send their children to school. "My younger daughter's elementary school was targeted for a suicide bombing," wrote Leitner. "They wanted to slip into the schoolyard during recess and blow themselves up among the children. These murderers were only caught (with their suicide belts and the map with the school) because of the [school's security] fence."[12]

Jewish Sabbath

For Christian Americans, the sabbath means a day off from work and perhaps an hour of church on Sunday. But the Jewish sabbath, called Shabbat, is much more involved. Shabbat lasts from sundown Friday to sundown Saturday. On Friday, observant Jews light candles, serve a special meal, and recite blessings. Jews attend services at the synagogue on Saturday. Throughout Shabbat, work is forbidden— even such activities as lawn care and driving a car.

▲ This family is participating in a traditional Passover seder meal.

In fact, public transportation and many stores and restaurants are closed during Shabbat.

▷ Major Holidays

Jews observe several major holidays. The High Holy Days in autumn begin with Rosh Hashanah (the Jewish New Year) and end ten days later with Yom Kippur. The High Holy Days are a time of repentance. Yom Kippur, the Day of Atonement, is the most sacred of Jewish holidays. In the spring, Jews celebrate Pesach (Passover). This eight-day holiday commemorates the exodus of the Hebrews from Egypt. Fifty days after Pesach comes Shavuot (Pentecost), which commemorates God's gift of the Torah and Commandments to Moses at Mount Sinai.

Each spring, Israelis honor two nonreligious holidays: Independence Day and Yom Hashoah (Holocaust Remembrance Day). At ten o'clock in the morning on Yom Hashoah, sirens wail throughout Israel. Everyone stops what he or she is doing (even driving) and stands in remembrance of Holocaust victims.

Most of us have heard about "keeping kosher," but what exactly does that mean? *Kashrut* is the body of Jewish law that deals with what foods Jews can eat and how those foods should be prepared and eaten. "Kosher" describes foods that meet these standards. According to the Book of Leviticus, the purpose of kashrut is holiness and ritual purity. The rules of kashrut are complex, but these are the basics:

Although bagels originated in Poland, they are a staple of the Israeli-Jewish diet. These bagels differ significantly from the ones that have become popular in the United States.

- Certain animals may not be eaten at any time, including pork and shellfish.

- Of those animals that may be eaten, the animals must be killed in accordance with Jewish law.

- All blood must be drained from the meat or broiled out of it before it is eaten.

- Certain parts of permitted animals may not be eaten.

- Meat cannot be eaten with dairy products.

- Utensils that have touched meat may not be used to eat dairy products.

- Grape products made by non-Jews may not be eaten.

Traditional Foods

Certain foods have been part of Jewish tradition for centuries. Bagels, for example, date back to the early 1600s in Poland. Challah is a sweet, eggy bread served during Shabbat and Jewish holidays. Other delicacies include gefilte fish (balls of chopped fish) and matzah ball soup (chicken soup with dumplings). Knishes are potato/flour mixtures stuffed with everything from cheese to chopped liver. Blintzes are like thin, rolled-up pancakes with filling—often fruit. They are great for breakfast or dessert.

Though not a traditional Jewish food, the shawarma is distinctively Israeli. Served in pita bread, it is filled with sliced lamb or chicken and such toppings as tomatoes, garlic sauce, pickles, and tabouli. "It's amazing how many shawarma kiosks

▲ *At the Western Wall in Jerusalem you can see the difference in clothing worn by the more conservative Jews in contrast to the more Westernized Jews.*

there are in Israel," wrote Meir Brooks. "I have seen a single block with three shawarma-selling kiosks on it! The people who make the shawarma are usually very social and talkative, and they share that unique friendship that most Israelis have."[13]

▶ Clothing

Most Israelis wear casual Western attire. However, strict Orthodox Jews wear distinct clothing. Orthodox men wear a black coat and a black, broad-brimmed hat. They also grow long sidelocks. Orthodox women always keep their heads covered.

During religious ceremonies, Jewish men wear a yarmulke, a small cap. The Orthodox wear the yarmulke every day, while the ultra-Orthodox Jews don a black cap. Clothing has become political. Many national religious Jews wear a white or light-colored crocheted yarmulke. Some Israelis casually refer to the ultra-Orthodox and national religious as "Black Hats" and "Crocheted Caps," respectively.

The Arts

From the earliest grades, Israeli students learn to appreciate music and the arts. And there is much to love. Many Israeli artists examine issues relating to Jewish identity and statehood. Yet Israeli art is wonderfully eclectic, reflecting the many cultures from where its people hail—be it from Western Europe, Russia, or North Africa. Russian Jew Marc Chagall, a famous twentieth-century artist, painted twelve windows on the synagogue at the Hadassah Hospital. The stained-glass windows depict the twelve tribes of Israel.

A nation of readers, Israel boasts hundreds of newspapers and magazines—as well as fine literature. Popular literary themes include Jewish identity, the problems and promise of the new state, and isolation of the individual. Writers Amos Oz and Shmuel Yosef Agnon are world-renowned.

Throughout Israel, the people celebrate all of the fine arts—from theater and opera to dance and classical music. The Israel Philharmonic Orchestra, in fact, is internationally famous. Native son Itzhak Perlman ranks among the greatest violinists in world history. America alone has showered him with fifteen Grammy awards.

▲ *Visitors can view and learn about the Dead Sea Scrolls at the Shrine of the Book in the Israel Museum in Jerusalem. This is an image of the shrine where many of the scrolls are on display.*

History is important to Israel, which may explain why the small nation boasts more than 120 museums. The Israel Museum in Jerusalem houses the Dead Sea Scrolls, important historical texts that date back more than two thousand years. In Jerusalem, the Yad Vashem Holocaust Museum is dedicated to Jews who died in the Holocaust. Jerusalem is also home to the Biblical Zoo. This popular tourist attraction features many species mentioned in the Bible.

▷ Sports

On the whole, Israel's young people are more fit than America's youth. Israelis take advantage of

Black September: Remembering the Tragedy of the Munich Olympics

ESPN.com: GEN - Keeping the torch lit - Microsoft Internet Explorer

File   Edit   View   Favorites   Tools   Help

Links »

Address http://espn.go.com/gen/s/2002/0903/1426796.html   Go

Continental Airlines   MORE POWER TO YOU.
                             Manage all your travel at continental.com.

ESPN Network: ESPN | NBA.com | NHL.com | ABC | Radio | EXPN | Insider | Shop | Fantasy

ESPN

BLACK SEPTEMBER
Remembering the Tragedy of the Munich Olympics

ESPN SEARCH   [   ]   Find

SPORT SECTIONS
MLB
Scores | GameCast
NFL
Scores
Col. Football
Scores
NBA
Scores
Golf
Scores
Tennis
Scores
Motorsports
Soccer
Boxing

Wednesday, September 4
Updated: September 5, 6:25 PM ET

Keeping the torch lit

By Tom Farrey
ESPN.com

SHAKER HEIGHTS, Ohio -- When the International Olympic Committee was asked to comment on its honoring of the 11 Israeli athletes and coaches slain on its watch, the introduction to the response, formed in an e-mail message, was as telling as any of the language that followed in the official statement.

"Please find hereunder the quote of the IOC President on Munich 1972," a spokesperson wrote.

Three decades later, time has reduced the tragedy to shorthand -- Munich 1972 -- a term that can only mean one thing. The terrorist killings remain the

More from ESPN...

At the Munich Olympic Games in 1972, eleven Israeli athletes and coaches were taken hostage and killed by Palestinian terrorists. Read more about this tragic event on this ESPN Web page.

Access this Web site from http://www.myreportlinks.com

the nation's many sports facilities. They participate in such activities as tennis, squash, soccer, and basketball. They also love to splash in the Mediterranean Sea and the country's many pools. Israelis, like most of the world, are passionate about soccer.

In thirteen Summer Olympic Games, Israel has won six medals—including a gold in windsurfing in 2004. However, even in sports Israel has experienced violence and tragedy. During the 1972 Munich Games, Palestinian terrorists massacred eleven Israeli athletes and coaches. It was just one of many, many atrocities in the four thousand-year history of the Jewish people.

Chapter 5 ▶

A Stateless People

Beginning in A.D. 70, the fate of Jews changed dramatically. That year, Romans destroyed the Second Temple in Jerusalem and starved or slaughtered an estimated six hundred thousand Jews. The Zealots, leaders of the Jews, fled to a mountaintop fortress called Masada. When besieged

▲ *The Church of the Nativity and Manger Square in Bethlehem. Christian worshippers of the Roman Empire ruled Jerusalem for centuries.*

by Roman troops, the Zealots committed mass suicide.

The surviving Jews dreamed of resurrecting the kingdom of Israel in Palestine (the Romans' name for the region). But their Roman rulers would have none of it. Romans quashed rebellions in A.D. 115 and 132, and in 135 they destroyed the central Jewish city of Jerusalem. Romans murdered thousands of Jews, and they sent most of the survivors to Roman colonies. Some fled to Europe and North Africa. Thus began the Diaspora, in which the Jews of Israel were forced to scatter around the world and ended up living in many separate communities.

▶ Palestine's Many Conquerors

In the 300s, the Roman Empire split in two: the Roman Empire in the West and the Byzantine Empire in the East. Under Emperor Constantine, the Roman Empire became Christianized. The Byzantines, who ruled Palestine, built churches in Jerusalem. They also constructed shrines in Jerusalem honoring Jesus, who had performed miracles in the area.

In the 600s, a new force emerged in the region. Arab Muslims, followers of the new religion Islam, captured Jerusalem from the Byzantines in 641. For the next four centuries, Arab Muslims ruled Palestine. They built mosques and shrines to Allah, with many in Jerusalem. According to Muslims,

Muhammad had dreamed that he ascended to Heaven from Jerusalem. Thus, Jews, Christians, and Muslims considered the city to be holy. Though Arabs ruled Palestine through the 1000s, they allowed Christians and the few Jews of Palestine to practice their own faiths.

In 1099, however, Christian Crusaders stormed Jerusalem and slaughtered Muslims and Jews. The Crusaders ruled Jerusalem until 1187, when it was recaptured by Muslims. In 1517, the Turkish Ottoman Empire took control of Palestine, and remained in power until World War I. During Ottoman rule, Arab Muslims were not allowed to serve in government. Jews and Christians had even fewer rights.

▶ European Jews Return to Palestine

From the 1000s to the 1600s, Jews in Europe were treated as outcasts and persecuted. According to *The Holocaust Chronicle,* Jews were viewed as "the devil's agents; Europe's greatest sinners . . . malicious murderers of Christian children . . . drinkers of Christian blood . . . and continued enemies of Jesus Christ."[1] Jews were falsely blamed (and murdered) for causing the bubonic plague in the 1300s. About one hundred thousand Jews were murdered in Poland and Russia in 1648–49.

Anti-Semitic (anti-Jewish) violence rose again in Europe in the late 1800s. At that point, some European Jews had had enough. In the early 1880s,

The Dome of the Rock, known to Muslims as Qubbat As-Sakhrah, is a sacred Islamic shrine.

Russian Jews began to immigrate into Palestine to escape persecution. This migration is called the First Aliyah (first migration), and the Jews called their destination Eretz Israel (land of Israel). The Jewish immigrants in Palestine farmed land that was sold to them by absentee Arab Palestinians. Just prior to the Jews' arrival, Palestine had a Jewish population of about twenty-five thousand, about 5 percent of the total population in the mostly Arab region. But that number soon swelled.

Zionism

In the mid-1890s, Zionism—the movement to unite Jews of the Diaspora and settle them in Palestine—led to increased immigration. In his book *The Jewish State,* Jewish journalist Theodor Herzl proposed the creation of a Jewish state in Palestine. In 1897 he convened the first Zionist Congress. The congress proposed Zionism's goal, which was "to create for the Jewish people a home in Palestine secured by Public Law."[2]

Around the world, hundreds of thousands of Jews donated money to the Zionist cause. From 1904 to 1914, in the Second Aliyah, about forty thousand Jews poured into Palestine, mostly from Eastern Europe. The Jewish community of Palestine was called the Yishuv. Some of the new settlers formed the city of Tel Aviv along the Mediterranean Sea. Many others formed kibbutzims.

This a photograph of Jewish colonies and settlements along Herzl Avenue in Tel Aviv in the 1920s. The street is named after journalist and philosopher Theodor Herzl.

The Arab residents of Palestine resented the new Jewish immigrants, who they felt were taking over their land. Moreover, the Ottomans still ruled over Palestine, and they refused to grant the Jews an autonomous state. At the onset of World War I, the fate of Palestine—and the Jews—was up in the air.

▶ WWI and the British Mandate

From 1914 to 1918, the Central Powers (Ottoman Empire, Germany, Austria-Hungary) waged war against the Allies (Great Britain, France, Russia, and later the United States). To get Arab support, the British vowed that they would uphold Arab independence in the Middle East if the Ottomans were defeated. Later, Arabs would claim that the deal included a promise of Arab independence in the Holy Land. The British would deny that they had made such a promise. In reality, Britain wanted to control Palestine itself.

Complicating matters, Britain in 1917 issued the Balfour Declaration. This stated that Britain "views with favor the establishment in Palestine of a national home for the Jewish people" as long as Jews and Palestine's half-million Arabs could peacefully share the land.[3] Historians believe Britain supported the Zionist cause in order to win Jews' support for the war effort. Whatever the reason, it was great news for the Jewish people.

World War I ended in 1918, with the Allies victorious. Two years later, the League of Nations gave

Britain a mandate (order) to administer Palestine until the territory's inhabitants were deemed ready for independence. In 1922 the region (what is now Israel, Gaza, West Bank, and Jordan) was split into two. The new Palestine, under British control, included only the western portion of the previous Palestine. The eastern territory became the independent Transjordan, ruled by Arabs.

During the 1920s, about one hundred thousand Jews immigrated to Palestine. By 1929 just about 20 percent of Palestine's eight hundred thousand or so citizens were Jewish. Many Arab landowners sold land to Jewish immigrants. This angered Arab peasants, who felt squeezed out. Arabs and Jews also bickered over the right to worship at the Western

BBC News: Middle East

This Web site from the BBC provides all the latest news from the Middle East, including Israel.

Access this Web site from http://www.myreportlinks.com

Wall. A remnant of the Second Temple, the Wall was also where Muhammad is said to have ascended to Heaven. During a week of Arab rioting in 1929, more than two hundred Jews and Arabs were killed.

The Rise of the Nazis

The situation worsened in 1933 when Adolf Hitler's Nazi Party took power in Germany. Anti-Semitism escalated in Germany and surrounding nations. By the tens of thousands, Jews—including doctors, lawyers, and other professionals—flocked to Palestine. Arab resentment of Jewish immigration swelled, too. In 1936, Arabs attacked Jewish businesses and farms, and British peacekeeping troops responded by killing more than a hundred Arabs. By 1939, death tolls rose into the thousands.

Throughout the interwar years (1918–39), the British allowed Jewish authorities to run their own internal affairs. The Jewish community elected a proto-government, the Jewish Agency. Under the Jewish Agency's guidance, Palestine's Jews built houses, schools, roads, hospitals, and agriculture settlements. They even created their own army, called the Haganah. With turmoil throughout the continent, the fate of Palestine was uncertain. But Jews were taking steps necessary to build their own nation. Arabs, meanwhile, were not nearly as well organized.

In 1937, Great Britain proposed to divide Palestine into two parts, with Arabs receiving 70 percent of the land and the Jews the rest. Arabs declined the offer. In 1939, the year that World War II began, Great Britain issued a White Paper, or official policy document. The order restricted Jewish immigration to Palestine to just seventy-five thousand total over the next five years. Zionists were furious with the decision.

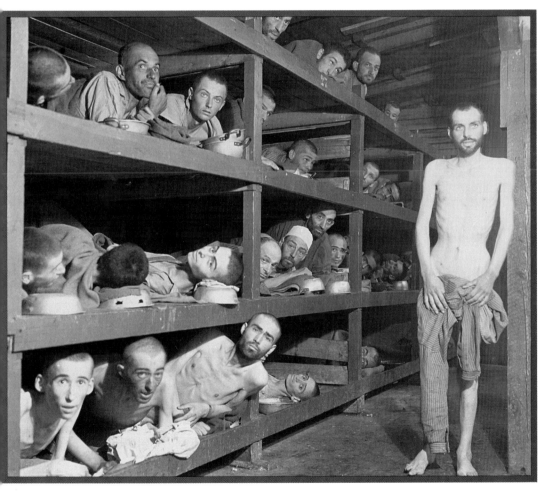

△ *This photo illustrates the cramped and horrific conditions at the Buchenwald concentration camp during the Holocaust. Nobel Prize-winning author Elie Wiesel was among the prisoners. He is in the second row from the bottom, seventh from the left.*

Leading up to World War II, many Europeans smoldered with anti-Semitism. In April 1938 alone, anti-Jewish riots swept Poland while a group of Jews in Vienna, Austria, were forced to eat grass. "By warding off the Jews," stated German leader Adolf Hitler, "I am fighting for the Lord's work."[4]

The Holocaust

On Hitler's orders, the Nazi regime carried out a systemic plan to murder the European Jewish population. As the German Army swept through Europe from 1939 to 1945, Jews were herded into ghettos and concentration camps. By the thousands, Jews died by machine-gun fire, starvation, overwork, death marches, or lethal gas administered in such death camps as Auschwitz. The endless list of atrocities included Nazis luring Jewish children into a pit with candy and then burying them alive.

Based on the White Paper, Jewish immigration to Palestine was illegal. However, Zionists chose to break the law rather than wait for extermination. During the war years, Zionists helped more than thirteen thousand Jews escape to Palestine.

By the time Germany was defeated in 1945, Nazis and their anti-Semitic collaborators had murdered approximately 6 million of the world's 19 million Jews. British Prime Minister Winston Churchill stated that "this is probably the greatest and most horrible crime ever committed in the whole history of the world. . . ."[5]

After the war, Holocaust survivors were left homeless, sickly, and emaciated. They were psychologically and spiritually devastated. Typically, they felt abandoned by their fellow human beings—and their God.

Throughout the Holocaust, the United States did little to help the Jews. However, in 1942, Zionists and non-Zionist organizations met in New York. In a statement known as the Biltmore Program, representatives publicly advocated the establishment of a Jewish commonwealth in Palestine.

Museum | Exhibitions - Microsoft Internet Explorer

File   Edit   View   Favorites   Tools   Help   Links »

Address http://www.ushmm.org/museum/exhibit/index.php?content=exhibit/   Go

MUSEUM I   N & DONATE

Done

In September 1941, the Nazis killed all thirty-five hundred Jewish residents of the town of Ejszyski, located in present-day Lithuania. The three-story-high Tower of Faces, shown here, displays over one thousand pictures taken between 1890 and 1941 of these victims of the Holocaust. Learn more about the Holocaust at the **United States Holocaust Memorial Museum** Web site.

After the war, about two hundred thousand Holocaust survivors lived in temporary camps for displaced persons. Britain still would not lift its restrictions to Palestine, so Zionists smuggled in tens of thousands of Holocaust survivors illegally. Right-wing Jewish groups, the Irgun and Lehi, wanted Britain out of Palestine completely. They bombed British targets, such as railroad lines, and assassinated British officials.

▲ The entrance to the Nazi concentration camp in Auschwitz, Poland. Auschwitz was one of the horrific Holocaust camps.

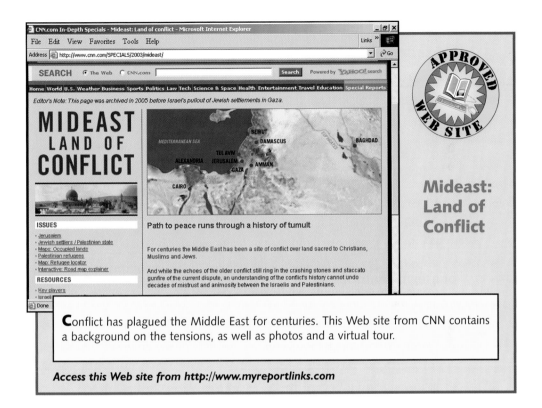

Conflict has plagued the Middle East for centuries. This Web site from CNN contains a background on the tensions, as well as photos and a virtual tour.

Access this Web site from http://www.myreportlinks.com

▷ **A Home for Jews**

By early 1947, Great Britain had grown weary of Palestine. In February, the British decided to refer the Palestine issue to the United Nations. A UN commission proposed that the region be partitioned into two states, one for Jews and one for Arabs. The recommended Jewish state would include the northern Galilee region, most of the Mediterranean coast, and most of the Negev Desert. The Arab state would include western and central areas of Galilee, part of the Negev Desert, the Gaza Strip, and an area east of the Jordan River now known as the West Bank.

By United Nations rules, the UN commission could only propose the plan, not enforce it. However, most countries, as well as most Jewish leaders, supported the plan. Arab Palestinians and surrounding Arab nations did not. After all, the six hundred thousand Jewish residents were getting close to 60 percent of the land. The 1.3 million Arabs in Palestine were getting only 40 percent. Arab Palestinians, in fact, wanted Palestine to be an Arab state entirely, with Jews as a minority.

Nevertheless, the UN passed the proposal, Resolution 181, on November 29, 1947. In response, the Arab League (which included Egypt, Iraq, Saudi Arabia, Transjordan, Yemen, Syria, and Lebanon) announced it would join with Arab Palestinians to oppose the UN resolution. Moreover, just hours after passage of the resolution, armed Arab Palestinians attacked Jewish towns and settlements. It became clear that anti-Jewish violence, prevalent since ancient times, was not about to end.

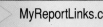

Chapter 6

An Embattled Nation

Although the UN resolution of November 1947 supported the creation of a Jewish state in Palestine, Jews had little chance to celebrate. Britain's mandate for the area would end on May 15, 1948, the day British troops would leave. Jews

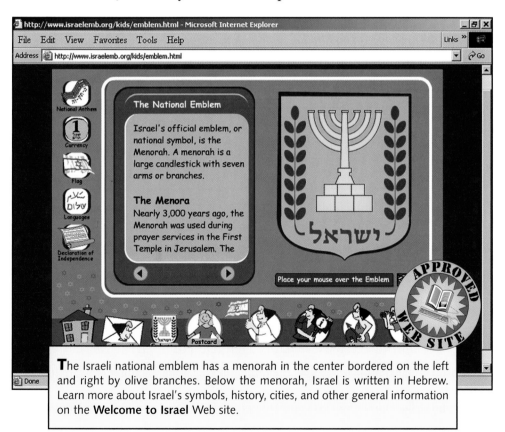

http://www.israelemb.org/kids/emblem.html - Microsoft Internet Explorer

File   Edit   View   Favorites   Tools   Help   Links »

Address http://www.israelemb.org/kids/emblem.html   Go

The National Emblem

Israel's official emblem, or national symbol, is the Menorah. A menorah is a large candlestick with seven arms or branches.

The Menora
Nearly 3,000 years ago, the Menorah was used during prayer services in the First Temple in Jerusalem. The

ישראל

Place your mouse over the Emblem

Done

The Israeli national emblem has a menorah in the center bordered on the left and right by olive branches. Below the menorah, Israel is written in Hebrew. Learn more about Israel's symbols, history, cities, and other general information on the **Welcome to Israel** Web site.

believed that at that time, the Arab League would attack.

Haganah, the Jewish Army, recruited thousands of fighters and armed them with weapons. They proceeded to occupy the territories that the UN had proposed should comprise the Jewish nation. By spring 1948, tens of thousands of Arabs had left those territories.

In May 1948, Jewish leaders in Palestine believed that their people were prepared for state-hood. The army had secured the proposed borders, and governmental and economic systems seemed solid. Moreover, the Jewish people were anxious and determined to finally have their own nation. Thus, on May 14, 1948, Jewish Palestinian leader David Ben-Gurion declared the establishment of the State of Israel. Other nations, most notably the United States and the Soviet Union, almost immediately recognized the new government.

▶ Arab Resistance

The Arab League, of course, did not. Within one day of Ben-Gurion's proclamation of independence, the Arab League declared war on the new state. The Arab-Israeli War (known as the War of Independence in Israel) raged for the next eight months. The new Israel Defense Force (IDF) battled troops from Egypt, Transjordan, Syria, Lebanon, and Iraq. Although each side boasted about eighty thou-sand troops, the IDF was much more organized and efficient. Over six thousand Israelis and an estimated eight thousand Arabs were killed in the war. Israel proved victorious by January 1949.

From February to July 1949, Israel and the Arab nations signed truce agreements that established new borders. Israel gained much more land, while Arab Palestinians wound up with no land at all. Transjordan (renamed Jordan in 1949) gained control of the large West Bank area, which had been allocated to Arab Palestinians in the 1947 UN resolution. Egypt took over the small Gaza Strip. Jerusalem was divided between Israel and Jordan. Finally, Israel took control of the Negev, all of Galilee, and a strip of land connecting the Mediterranean Sea to Jerusalem.

Arab Palestinians, now homeless, had to decide their own fate. Close to 150,000 Arabs remained in the territory that was now Israel, and they were granted Israeli citizenship. Hundreds of thousands moved to Jordan's West Bank or Egypt's Gaza Strip. Others fled to Jordan, Syria, and Lebanon. Still more settled in UN-funded refugee camps, waiting for a better life.

Israel Grows Up

Israel emerged from the war with thousands of wounded soldiers and a huge national debt. However, Israeli citizens were determined to make their new nation work. In 1949, Israelis held their first national election, as they chose their country's

ISRAEL MINISTRY OF FOREIGN AFFAIRS

Israel Ministry of Foreign Affairs: Historical Overview

MFA > History of Israel > Historical overview

Facts About Israel- History (4 Feb 2004)

HISTORY- Biblical Times (3 Feb 2004)

HISTORY- The Second Temple (3 Feb 2004)

This Web site from the Israel Ministry of Foreign Affairs provides an overview of the nation's history.

EDITOR'S CHOICE

Access this Web site from http://www.myreportlinks.com

first Knesset. David Ben-Gurion was named prime minister and Chaim Weizmann president.

The new government recognized the importance of Judaism to the nation. As a result, Saturday was declared a national day of rest, with businesses and public transportation shut down. Moreover, some tax money would support religious schools, and devoutly religious Jews would be exempt from military service. The new government also guaranteed liberty and equal rights for its citizens, including Arab Israelis.

Israel also welcomed all Jewish immigrants. Holocaust survivors living in displaced-persons camps in Europe arrived in large numbers. So, too, did Jews from Arab nations who had experienced persecution largely because of the Arab-Israeli War. From 1948 to 1951, more than six hundred thousand Jewish immigrants arrived in Israel, doubling the country's Jewish population. Financial aid from the United States and West Germany helped Israel build its economy. The government wisely invested funds in agriculture, infrastructure, mining, and industry. Working together, the Israeli people were determined to build a strong, prosperous nation.

The Suez Crisis

Though armistices (war-ending agreements) had been signed by Israel and Arab nations in 1949, official peace treaties had not been. Arabs refused to sign such treaties until Palestinian refugees were allowed to return to their homes and Israel pulled back its borders in accordance with the 1947 UN partition plan. Palestinian guerrillas, armed by Egypt, launched sustained attacks against Israel. Among Arab nations, Egypt emerged as Israel's chief enemy.

In 1954, Egyptian leader Gamal Abdel-Nasser blocked Israel's shipping route through the Strait of Tiran. Two years later, Nasser took control of the Suez Canal. Although it was in Nasser's country, Britain and France had long controlled the canal. With mutual anger toward Egypt, Britain and France stormed the Suez Canal Zone in fall 1956 and seized control of the precious waterway. Meanwhile, Israeli

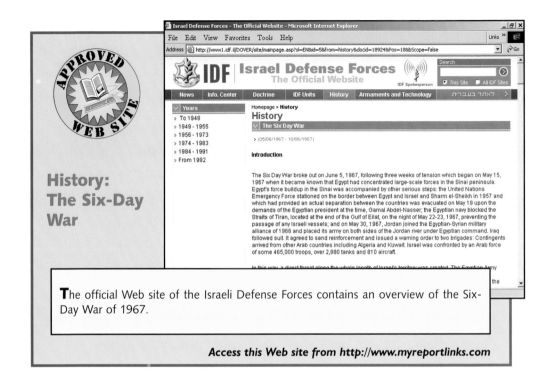

Israel Defense Forces — The Official Website — Microsoft Internet Explorer

File   Edit   View   Favorites   Tools   Help   Links »

Address http://www1.idf.il/DOVER/site/mainpage.asp?sl=EN&id=S&from=history&docid=18924&Pos=18&bScope=false   Go

IDF | Israel Defense Forces
The Official Website
IDF Spokesperson   Search   This Site   All IDF Sites

News | Info. Center | Doctrine | IDF Units | History | Armaments and Technology | לאתר בעברית

Years
> To 1948
> 1949 - 1955
> 1956 - 1973
> 1974 - 1983
> 1984 - 1991
> From 1992

Homepage > **History**

History

The Six Day War

> (05/06/1967 - 10/06/1967)

Introduction

The Six Day War broke out on June 5, 1967, following three weeks of tension which began on May 15, 1967 when it became known that Egypt had concentrated large-scale forces in the Sinai peninsula. Egypt's force buildup in the Sinai was accompanied by other serious steps: the United Nations Emergency Force stationed on the border between Egypt and Israel and Sharm el-Sheikh in 1957 and which had provided an actual separation between the countries was evacuated on May 19 upon the demands of the Egyptian president at the time, Gamal Abdel-Nasser; the Egyptian navy blocked the Straits of Tiran, located at the end of the Gulf of Eilat, on the night of May 22-23, 1967, preventing the passage of any Israeli vessels; and on May 30, 1967, Jordan joined the Egyptian-Syrian military alliance of 1966 and placed its army on both sides of the Jordan river under Egyptian command. Iraq followed suit. It agreed to send reinforcement and issued a warning order to two brigades: Contingents arrived from other Arab countries including Algeria and Kuwait. Israel was confronted by an Arab force of some 465,000 troops, over 2,880 tanks and 810 aircraft.

In this way, a direct threat along the whole length of Israel's territory was created. The Egyptian Army

The official Web site of the Israeli Defense Forces contains an overview of the Six-Day War of 1967.

Access this Web site from http://www.myreportlinks.com

forces conquered the Sinai Peninsula. The action, however, was condemned by the United States and the Soviet Union. Under pressure, the three nations returned the canal and Sinai to Egypt.

After the crisis, Arab-Israeli hostilities lessened. Into the 1960s, Israel forged strong relations with Western nations, and its economy prospered. In 1964, however, the Arab League created the Palestine Liberation Organization (PLO), which encouraged Palestinian nationalist activities. A year later, Palestinians began armed attacks against Israel. Hostilities escalated, as Israel responded with raids against Syria and Jordan.

The Six-Day War

In 1967, the crisis reached full boil when it was reported falsely that Israel was amassing a larger number of troops near its border with Syria. Egypt's Nasser was furious with Israel about its supposed buildup. In response, Nasser reestablished the blockade at the Strait of Tiran, and he formed a mutual defense pact with Syria, Iraq, and Jordan. He also amassed troops on the Egyptian-Israeli border. Believing that they would soon be attacked, Israeli leaders acted first.

On June 5, 1967, Israeli forces led by Chief of Staff and General Yitzhak Rabin destroyed the entire Egyptian Air Force. They also decimated much of Jordan's and Syria's air power. Over the next six days, Israeli ground forces moved at will into hostile territories. By the time the Six-Day War had ended, Israel had conquered the Golan Heights from Syria, the Gaza Strip and large Sinai Peninsula from Egypt, and the West Bank and East Jerusalem from Jordan. Israel actually tripled its territory. Israeli casualties totaled 759 dead and about 3,000 wounded. There are no exact figures for the Arab dead and wounded, but it is estimated that Egypt, Jordan, and Syria suffered a total of ten thousand to fifteen thousand casualties. Egypt's losses were by far the heaviest.

All of a sudden, Israel controlled territories in which one million Palestinians lived. Israeli leaders decided to retain all of Jerusalem and proclaim it Israel's capital. They also made it clear that they

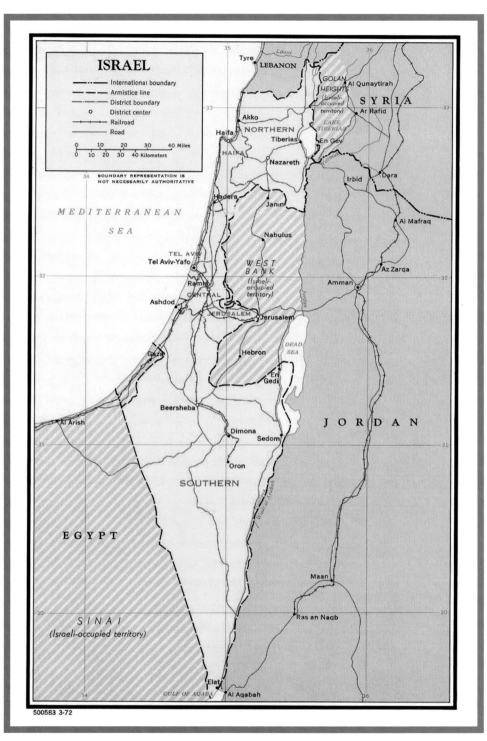

ISRAEL

- ········· International boundary
- ─ ─ ─ Armistice line
- ─·─·─ District boundary
- ○ District center
- ┼─┼─┼ Railroad
- ─── Road

0 10 20 30 40 Miles
0 10 20 30 40 Kilometers

BOUNDARY REPRESENTATION IS
NOT NECESSARILY AUTHORITATIVE

Tyre
LEBANON
Litani

GOLAN
HEIGHTS
(Israeli-
occupied
territory)
Al Qunaytirah
SYRIA
Ar Rafid

Akko
NORTHERN
LAKE
TIBERIAS
En Gev

Haifa
HAIFA
Tiberias
Yarmuk

Nazareth
Irbid
Dara

MEDITERRANEAN
SEA

Hadera
Janin
Al Mafraq

Nabulus

TEL AVIV
Tel Aviv-Yafo
WEST
BANK
(Israeli-
occupied
territory)

Ramle
CENTRAL
Jordan
Amman
Az Zarqa

Ashdod
JERUSALEM
Jerusalem

Gaza
Hebron
DEAD
SEA

Beersheba
En
Gedi

Al Arish
JORDAN

Dimona
Sedom

Oron

SOUTHERN

EGYPT
Wadi al Arabah

Maan

SINAI
(Israeli-occupied territory)
Ras an Naqb

Elat
GULF OF AQABA
Al Aqabah

500583 3-72

▲ *This map shows Israel and the territories it occupied after the 1967 Six-Day War and other wars with Arab nations.*

would trade the newly conquered territory for peace treaties with their Arab neighbors. Arab countries, however, refused to recognize Israel as a legitimate state. Hence, they rejected the "land for peace" proposal.

Many Israelis favored keeping the occupied territories since the land provided a safe buffer zone from enemies. While Israel did not officially annex the territories, it did establish settlements in them. Housing, roads, and businesses were built in these regions. Moreover, Israel offered health care and low-scale jobs to the Palestinians in the territories.

▶ War and Peace

In general, most Palestinians were unhappy living as stateless people in Israeli-occupied territory. Some Palestinians, living in the West Bank were, for the time being, subjects of the country of Jordan. In the late 1960s, the PLO—led by Yasser Arafat—rose to prominence. This organization represented the displaced Palestinians and its enemy was Israel. Relentlessly, the PLO launched terrorist attacks, including airplane hijackings and bombings of public places.

Meanwhile, Arab nations remained hostile toward Israel because the Israeli government refused to discuss returning the occupied territories. In 1969, President Nasser of Egypt launched the War of Attrition against its neighbor, which the Israelis withstood. Then in 1973, on the Jewish holy day of

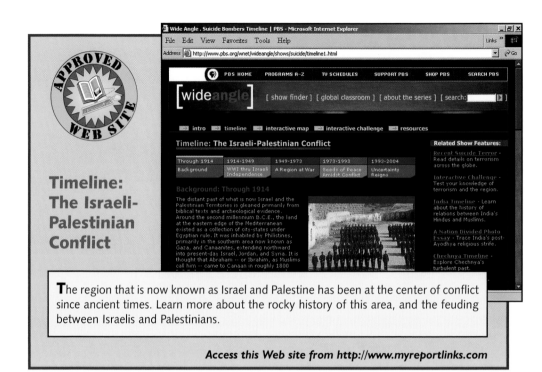

Timeline:
The Israeli-
Palestinian
Conflict

The region that is now known as Israel and Palestine has been at the center of conflict since ancient times. Learn more about the rocky history of this area, and the feuding between Israelis and Palestinians.

Access this Web site from http://www.myreportlinks.com

Yom Kippur, Egypt and Syria attacked Israeli positions in the Golan Heights and the Sinai Peninsula. Israelis recovered to drive out the enemy, but they suffered heavy losses.

After the War of 1973, also called the Yom Kippur War, Israel took a more hard-line stance against its Arab neighbors. The right-wing Likud Party rose to power, headed by Menachem Begin. The new government aggressively established new settlements in the occupied territories. From the mid-1970s to the early 1980s, the number of Jews living in the West Bank rose from five thousand to a hundred thousand. Cheap housing and appealing tax breaks awaited those who settled in the West

Bank. Many religious Israelis believed that Jews were entitled to the land, because it had been theirs during biblical times.

In the late 1970s, Egyptian President Anwar Sadat became the first Arab leader to extend a friendly hand to Israel. In a March 1979 ceremony in the United States, Egypt and Israel signed a formal peace agreement known as the Camp David Accords. Egypt regained the Sinai Peninsula in exchange for a promise of peace and diplomatic relations with Israel.

Syria, though, remained an adversary. Israel refused to return the Golan Heights unconditionally to Syria, and in fact, Israel officially annexed the territory in 1981. Nor would Begin appease Arafat's PLO, which represented the Palestinians. Begin considered the PLO as nothing more than a terrorist organization.

▶ War in Lebanon

Since 1970, the PLO had been headquartered in Lebanon, Israel's neighbor to the north. For more than a decade, PLO guerrillas attacked Israel from this strategic location. By 1982, after a PLO military buildup near the Israeli border, Begin had had enough. Israeli forces, led by Defense Minister Ariel Sharon, proceeded to destroy PLO military bases in southern Lebanon.

Moving northward in Lebanon to Beirut, Israeli soldiers shelled PLO targets for two months in 1982.

▲ *Ariel Sharon (front right) was in charge of Israeli forces during the invasion of Lebanon. This photo was taken on June 15, 1982.*

Reckless in their pursuit, they killed an estimated sixty-seven hundred people in Beirut, most of whom were civilians. The operation did indeed flush the PLO out of Lebanon. However, most of the world was outraged by Israel's actions. Many Israelis protested the war in large demonstrations. In the aftermath, Prime Minister Begin resigned.

▶ The Intifada

By 1987, Palestinians felt more powerless than ever. The PLO had moved its headquarters all the way to North Africa, and Israel continued to strengthen its settlements in the occupied territories. Beginning in late 1987, an intifada (Arabic for uprising) arose. Palestinians staged boycotts and strikes. They shut down businesses, and Palestinian children threw rocks at Israeli soldiers. As the intifada lasted into the early 1990s, Israelis felt a need to broker peace with the Palestinians.

Though the PLO was not involved initially in the intifada, it did step forward to represent the leadership of the uprising. The PLO gained more clout in 1988 when Jordan renounced its claim to the West Bank feeling the claim should belong to the PLO. Meanwhile, some Palestinians became more realistic in their goals. Instead of reclaiming all of Palestine from the Jews, they would accept a smaller Palestinian state—in the West Bank and Gaza.

In 1992, Israeli citizens voted the Labor Party to power. The country's new prime minister, Yitzhak Rabin, was determined to work for peace with the Palestinians. For the first time since the PLO's inception in 1964, Israel agreed to negotiate with what it had used to dismiss as a terrorist organization.

▶ Peace Attempts With the PLO

In 1993, Israel and the PLO each made unprecedented concessions. Israel recognized the PLO as the

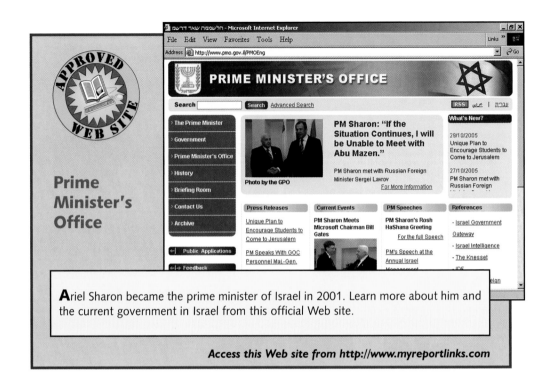

Ariel Sharon became the prime minister of Israel in 2001. Learn more about him and the current government in Israel from this official Web site.

Access this Web site from http://www.myreportlinks.com

representative of the Palestinian people, and the PLO confirmed Israel's right to exist in peace and security. The PLO renounced the use of terrorism and supported peaceful negotiations with Israel.

On September 13, 1993, in Washington, Rabin and Arafat outlined a proposal. Palestinians would have limited self-rule in the Gaza Strip as well as in the West Bank town of Jericho. The agreement also stated that the two sides would reach a comprehensive peace settlement regarding all remaining issues in dispute. They also agreed that the Palestinian Authority (PA) would administer these regions.

In 1994 and 1995, the two sides agreed on further issues, such as taxation and education for

Palestinians. In 1996, Arafat was elected leader of the Palestinian Authority. Another breakthrough came in 1994 when Israel and Jordan signed a peace treaty.

Not all Israelis, however, supported the peace process. Jews living in the West Bank feared that their settlements would be dismantled, with the land given to Palestinians. Many religious Israelis believed that all of Israel's territory belonged to the Jews. Yigal Amir was one Israeli college student who opposed the peace process. On November 4, 1995, he assassinated Prime Minister Rabin.

▶ Extremists Stir Things Up

The new prime minister, Shimon Peres, vowed to work for peace. However, two Palestinian extremist groups—Hamas and Islamic Jihad—also strove to sabotage negotiations. These groups did not want compromise, believing that all of Israel belonged to Arab Palestinians and that they should fight to reclaim it. In 1995 and 1996, Hamas and Islamic Jihad terrorized Israel with a succession of suicide bombings. On February 25, 1996, for example, two Hamas suicide bombers exploded themselves on a bus in Jerusalem, killing twenty-seven civilians.

Feeling angry and betrayed, Israelis voted for hard-liner Binyamin Netanyahu as prime minister in 1996. Netanyahu insisted that the PA work to

▲ Bystanders and Israeli soldiers come to the aid of a victim of the suicide bombing that occurred in downtown Jerusalem on February 25, 1996.

prevent terrorism before Israel would make any more concessions.

▶ New Agreements

Nevertheless, under international pressure, Netanyahu did resume talks with Arafat in 1997. The following year, he signed the Wye River Memorandum. Israel agreed to withdraw from 13 percent of the West Bank—in addition to the 27 percent that they had already withdrawn from—if the Palestinian leadership agreed to help prevent attacks on Israelis. Over time, according to the memorandum, about 40 percent of the West Bank (where the great majority of Palestinians lived) would be under the control of the PA.

As it turned out, Netanyahu ceded only some of the promised territory to the PA. Frustrated with their leader's reluctance to push for peace, Israelis voted for the Labor Party's Ehud Barak as prime minister in the 1999 election.

Barak vs. Arafat

Barak was determined to hammer out a peace agreement. In the summer of 2000, he met with

Beginning in 1993, Israel and Palestinian Authority participated in talks to bring peace to the Middle East. Years went by, and the talks ultimately failed in 2002. Learn more from this PBS Web site.

Access this Web site from http://www.myreportlinks.com

Arafat and U.S. President Bill Clinton at Camp David in the United States. Barak made what most felt was a generous offer: Israel would withdrawal from more than 90 percent of the West Bank and all of the Gaza Strip if the Palestinians would formerly renounce their demands to return to Israel. Yet Arafat rejected the offer. He believed that all Palestinians (and their descendants) who were forced to flee their homeland since the first Arab-Israeli War of 1948 should be allowed to return.

▶ Stalemate

Arafat's demand was highly impractical to Israel. It meant that more than 3 million Arabs—in refugee camps in the West Bank and Gaza as well as in Arab nations—could return to land that was now part of Israel. Besides the near impossibility of supporting such huge numbers, Israel would become a largely Arab state.

Barak proposed that Arab refugees could settle in a new Palestinian state comprised of the occupied territory that Israel was ceding to the PA. Barak also suggested that refugees in other Arab countries could be granted full citizenship in those countries and financially compensated by the international community.

Arafat refused the offer. Months later, Israeli and Palestinian negotiators met again in Egypt. Barak offered the PA more land in the West Bank as well as more control over holy sites in Jerusalem. Again, no deal was made—much to the frustration of both Israelis and Palestinians.

The Second Intifada

In September 2000, Likud leader Ariel Sharon made a controversial visit to the Temple Mount in Jerusalem. On the site, he proclaimed the area as eternal Israeli territory. Many Palestinians were furious with Sharon, and the next day rioting broke out in Jerusalem. Some believe this rioting was planned. Soon, more rioting erupted in the West Bank and Gaza, triggering the second intifada.

Palestinian militants are considered a threat to Israel's national security. In response, the Jewish state has taken what many consider to be extreme measures, which often result in a great number of deaths. Read the latest news from Israel and the rest of the Middle Eastern region on the **Israel Daily** Web site.

Israeli police cracked down hard. In the first week of the intifada, more than sixty Palestinians were killed and more than two thousand were injured.

With tensions high again, Israelis elected the hard-line Sharon as prime minister in February 2001. Meanwhile, Palestinian extremist groups rained terror on Israel with a rash of suicide bombings. On June 1, 2001, for example, a Hamas suicide bomber killed twenty-one Israelis in a dance club.

▶ The World's Concern

On September 11, 2001, the Islamic terrorist group al-Qaeda launched attacks in the United States that killed approximately three thousand people. Al-Qaeda leader Osama Bin Laden, an enemy of Israel and Western influence in the Arab world, promised more major assaults. Bin Laden has said that al-Qaeda will attack any nation that supports Israel. Before and after 9/11, al-Qaeda and other Islamic terrorist groups launched attacks around the globe. Thus, Israeli-Arab relations became a grave concern for every nation.

In 2001, Sharon believed Arafat was involved in terrorist activities. As a result, Israeli troops surrounded Arafat's West Bank headquarters in Ramallah, containing Arafat from October 2001 to April 2002. Meanwhile, on March 27, 2002, a suicide bomber killed thirty Israelis in a hotel restaurant during Passover.

BBC NEWS - Microsoft Internet Explorer

File   Edit   View   Favorites   Tools   Help   Links »

Address http://news.bbc.co.uk/1/shared/spl/hi/middle_east/04/bomb_attack_survivor/html/1.stm   Go

bbc.co.uk   Home TV Radio Talk Where I Live A-Z Index   Search

Low Graphics version | Change edition   Contact us | Help

BBCNEWS UK EDITION   WATCH BBC NEWS IN VIDEO

News Front Page
World
UK
England
Northern Ireland
Scotland
Wales
Business
Politics
Health
Education
Science/Nature
Technology
Entertainment

Have Your Say
Magazine
In Pictures

Photo journal: Bomb attack survivor

Introduction

As part of a series of photo journals about ordinary people's experiences, BBC News Online looks at the life of a survivor of a suicide bomb attack in Israel.

Elad Wafa lives in N...
He is 27 years o...
Ethiopia. On th...
May 2002, a P...
bomber let of...
the vegetable...
worked.

Elad suffered se...
now paralysed fro...

An explosion by a Palestinian suicide bomber left Elad Wafa, an African Jew, paralyzed from the lower back down with scars all over his face and arms. Although his physical challenges frustrate Elad, he is considered lucky that he still has his life. Read about Israeli-Palestinian relations on the **In Depth: Israel and the Palestinians** Web site from the BBC.

APPROVED WEB SITE

EDITOR'S CHOICE

Sharon retaliated against the bombings with "Operation Defensive Shield." Israeli troops stormed the West Bank in search of terrorist targets. They bombed weapons factories and apprehended suspected militants, while some Palestinians fought back. Several hundred Palestinians were killed during the operation.

Peace efforts were made in 2002 and 2003, but with little success. At an Arab League summit conference in March 2002, the league endorsed a plan to recognize Israel in exchange for the end of all occupation. Sharon found the proposal unacceptable. In 2003 the United States, the United Nations, Britain, and the European Union proposed a "Roadmap to Peace" for Israel and Palestine.

Meir Brooks of Haifa discussed the frustration of all the failed peace talks. "Each side was thinking how they could further their own goals and give the other side as little as possible," he wrote. "Also, they had no problem leaving negotiations at a dead end, no problem with threatening to end the talks should their standards not be met. The two sides didn't consider enough the alternative, the horrible alternative of keeping the status quo."[1]

In 2003, peace seemed far from reach. Suicide bombings continued while Israel moved to assassinate terrorist leaders. Israel, moreover, confiscated additional Palestinian lands and began construction of a large "security fence" in the West Bank. In July 2004, the UN Court of Justice gave its opinion that the barrier violated international law and had to be torn down. Upcoming weeks saw more suicide bombings, an assassination of a Hamas leader, and disagreement in the Knesset about Israeli withdrawal in occupied territories.

Fifty-six years had passed since the formation of Israel. Yet for its troubled citizens, peace remained an elusive dream.

A Strained Economy

All factors considered, it is extraordinary that Israelis enjoy a relatively high standard of living. With the nation in a constant state of war and surrounded by historically hostile neighbors, Israel must devote much of its budget to military and security. According to the *2005 CIA World Factbook,* Israel devotes $1,467 per person to military expenditures.[1]

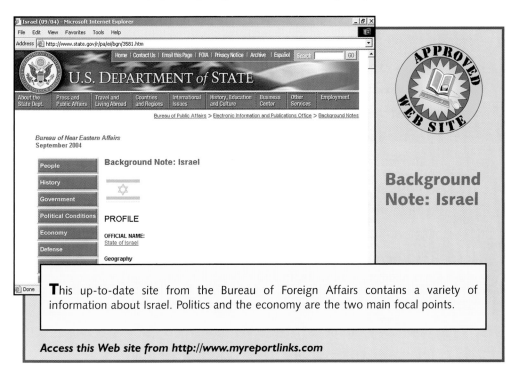

Background Note: Israel

This up-to-date site from the Bureau of Foreign Affairs contains a variety of information about Israel. Politics and the economy are the two main focal points.

Access this Web site from http://www.myreportlinks.com

No other nation in the world spends even one thousand dollars per person on national defense.

Moreover, immigration is another unique economic challenge that Israel has faced. All Jews are welcome, and with the collapse of the Soviet Union, hundreds of thousands of Jews from Eastern Europe immigrated to Israel in the 1990s. The Israeli government provides immigrants with housing, education, and job training.

Despite these tax burdens, the Israeli economy is in good shape. The nation's gross domestic product (GDP) per capita in 2002 was $19,500, which ranked fortieth out of 230 nations. Economists credit Israel's success to producing a wide variety of goods and services, investments, a skilled and educated workforce, and a commitment to research and development.

▶ **Division of Labor**

Most Israelis are well educated, and they hope to enter lucrative fields. Good jobs, however, are hard to find. "You must be highly educated and motivated, and a little luck would help," wrote Shelley Yachbesh of Moshav Neve Yamin, Israel.[2] Unemployment in the country is also high—typically around 10 percent.

All told, close to 3 million Israelis comprise the country's labor force (about 250,000 of whom are Arab Israelis). Approximately 180,000 Israelis serve in the military. The Histadrut Union (General

Federation of Labor) represents most of Israel's labor force.

The large influx of Eastern European immigrants in the 1990s became a sore spot among Palestinians. The new Jewish citizens took many of the low-paying, manual-labor jobs that Palestinian workers had relied upon. The situation added more fuel to the Arab-Israeli tensions.

▲ A banana plantation in Israel. Fruit harvesting and production is one of Israel's largest agricultural industries.

▶ Israeli Industries

About 70 percent of Israelis work in the service sector. The government funds such major service industries as education, health, and welfare. Other people work in the fields of business and finance, wholesale and retail trade, transportation, and communication.

Since the beginning of Zionism, Israelis have placed a strong emphasis on agriculture. Only about 3 percent of the workforce toils in agriculture, but Israel produces most of the food it needs. About 750 kibbutzim and moshavim produce a large portion of the nation's crops.

Israel's agricultural products include cotton, sugar beets, ground nuts, cereals, tomatoes, fruit, dairy products, poultry, and eggs. Its exports include fruit, cotton, avocados, and potatoes—as well as flowers. Israel gets most of its edible fish from human-made freshwater ponds.

Israel's industrial sector helps drive the nation's economy. Manufacturing employs about 28 percent of the workforce and accounts for about 80 percent of the nation's export earnings. Israel's manufacturing sector, located primarily in Tel Aviv and Haifa, is the most diversified and most advanced in the Middle East.

Traditionally, Israel's manufacturing focused on food processing, textiles, chemicals, pharmaceuticals, and metal products. In recent decades, the nation has advanced to high-tech fields, including medical electronics, computers, telecommunications, and diamond polishing.

Mining is an important aspect of the industrial sector. From the salt deposits of the Dead Sea, workers mine bromine, potash, magnesium, and other minerals. Miners who toil in the heat of the Negev extract copper, phosphates, bromine, and clay.

Tourism

In 2000, which was a great year for tourism in Israel, 2.5 million tourists poured $3 billion into the nation's economy. Typically, more than half of

http://www.goisrael.com/IMOTroot/images/WallPaper/wallpaper6.bmp - Microsoft Internet Explorer

File Edit View Favorites Tools Help   Links »

Address http://www.goisrael.com/IMOTroot/images/WallPaper/wallpaper6.bmp   Go

Ruins of the acropolis still stand at Avdat, an ancient city located in the Negev 40 miles south of Beersheba. Learn more about Israel's major tourist attractions at the **Israel: No One Belongs Here More Than You** Web site.

Israel's visitors come from Western Europe. However, during periods of political unrest and terrorist attacks, tourism drops significantly. When that happens, the economy is negatively affected.

Most tourists find Israel to be an unforgettable— sometimes life-changing—experience. "There are many, many sites that are precious to Christians," wrote Naomi Leitner, "since this is where Jesus was born and preached and was crucified."[3] Jewish tourists tend to visit the holy city of Jerusalem as well as Masada, where the Zealots met their fate.

Other tourists, wrote Mitchell Bard, executive director of the American-Israeli Cooperative Enterprise, "go to Caeserea for archeology . . . Safed for mysticism, Golan Heights for geography and beauty . . . Dead Sea for uniqueness . . . and [Elat] for spectacular sea."[4] Tel Aviv boasts glorious beaches and New York-style nightlife. Visitors to Haifa stop at the Baha'i gardens and marvel at the array of trees, flowers, and fountains. "At night," wrote Meir Brooks of Haifa, "the gardens light up in a truly great spectacle."[5]

▶ Transportation and Energy

Bus service for the people of Israel is well developed and runs smoothly. However, with terrorists targeting buses in recent years, more commuters began driving to work. This development worsened Israel's already notorious traffic problem. "Oy, just get in a car," wrote Bard. "Far more Israelis die in traffic accidents than terror attacks."[6]

Many Israeli drivers are aggressive and reckless, perhaps—some claim—because of the tensions in the country. Also, parking and traffic are often a problem caused by congested cities with narrow streets. "Many of the old cities, such as Tel Aviv and Jerusalem, don't have room to expand infrastructure," Bard wrote.[7]

Unlike its Middle Eastern neighbors, Israel produces only small amounts of oil and natural gas. Israel imports its oil from Egypt and Mexico, and it obtains its coal from South Africa, Australia, and the United Kingdom. Israel is always striving to develop alternative sources of energy. It is at the forefront in

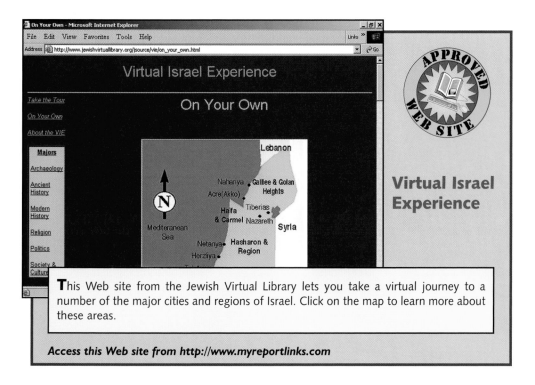

This Web site from the Jewish Virtual Library lets you take a virtual journey to a number of the major cities and regions of Israel. Click on the map to learn more about these areas.

Access this Web site from http://www.myreportlinks.com

Haifa, along the beautiful Mediterranean coast, is Israel's third-largest city.

the development of solar energy, especially solar panels for home water heating.

Communication and Media

Israel is a high-tech, well-connected country. In fact, it boasts as many cellular phones as people. Citizens also take advantage of the Internet and e-mail.

The media in Israel is granted freedom of speech. Israel boasts more than two dozen daily newspapers, about half in Hebrew. Daily papers include *Ha'aretz, Yedioth Ahronoth, Ma'ariv,* and the English-language *Jerusalem Post.*

The Israeli Broadcasting Authority (IBA) operates public radio and television stations, while the state-run Kol Israel manages several radio stations. Also, since 1993, Israel has allowed commercial television. Most households get cable with several dozen channels to choose from. Like Americans, Israelis can flip on sports, nature, music, movies, and children's channels.

Potential for Prosperity

Throughout its history, Israel has welcomed foreign aid and loans—particularly from the United States—to sustain itself. All told, the United States has given Israel tens of billions of dollars in assistance. Israel's government and citizenry, a proud people, hope the days of financial dependence will eventually end.

Financial independence could come if peace could be achieved. If the Israeli government reaches agreements with the Palestinian Authority—and militant groups lay down their weapons—prosperity would follow. Funds for security and the military could be lowered. Foreign investment would improve, and tourism would flourish.

There have been promising signs. In February 2005, after peace prospects improved due to the death of PA leader Yasser Arafat, Israeli stocks skyrocketed. "Israeli stocks are doing better not just because of the political situation improving, but also because they are concentrated in areas like telephony and Internet technology, and pharmaceuticals, which are good sectors to be in right now," said Vivian Lewis, editor of *Global Investing*. "The politics can only help."[8]

Citizens hope that with real peace, Israel would become a great and prosperous nation. "Our economy would most definitely boom," wrote Israeli citizen Shelley Yachbesh. "Think of all the money that could be spent on education, medicine, etc., and not on security. Think of how much money the army alone would save."[9]

Naomi Leitner, recognizing Israel's great beauty, culture, and heritage, summed it up. "With a little peace," she wrote, "this country would be one of the wonders of the world."[10]

		STOP						
Back	Forward	Stop	Review	Home	Explore	Favorites	History

Report Links

The Internet sites described below can be accessed at http://www.myreportlinks.com

▶***The World Factbook:* Israel**
Editor's Choice Learn more about Israel from this CIA Web site.

▶**Perry-Castañeda Library Map Collection: Israel Maps**
Editor's Choice View historical and present-day maps of Israel.

▶**In Depth: Israel and the Palestinians**
Editor's Choice Find out about the shaky relationship between Israelis and Palestinians.

▶**Israel Ministry of Foreign Affairs: Historical Overview**
Editor's Choice An overview of Israeli history.

▶***Israel Daily***
Editor's Choice Get daily news from this Israeli newspaper.

▶**Religion & Ethics: Judaism**
Editor's Choice Learn more about the Jewish religion from this online resource.

▶**The American Israel Public Affairs Committee**
The American Israel Public Affairs Committee works to further pro-Israeli interests.

▶**Background Note: Israel**
Travelers to Israel should check out this site from the U.S. Department of State.

▶**BBC News: Middle East**
Get the latest news coming out of the Middle East.

▶**Black September: Remembering the Tragedy of the Munich Olympics**
Read about the terrorist attack against Israelis at the 1972 Olympics.

▶**Heritage: Civilization and the Jews**
This Web site provides an extensive overview of Jewish history.

▶**History: The Six Day War**
In 1967, Israel attacked Egyptian, Jordanian, and Syrian forces.

▶**In Depth: Death of Arafat**
Extensive coverage of Yasser Arafat's death and a summary of his legacy.

▶**InfoNation Advanced**
The United Nations provides statistics on countries from around the world.

▶**Israel: No One Belongs Here More Than You**
The official Israeli tourism Web site provides information for those traveling to the country.

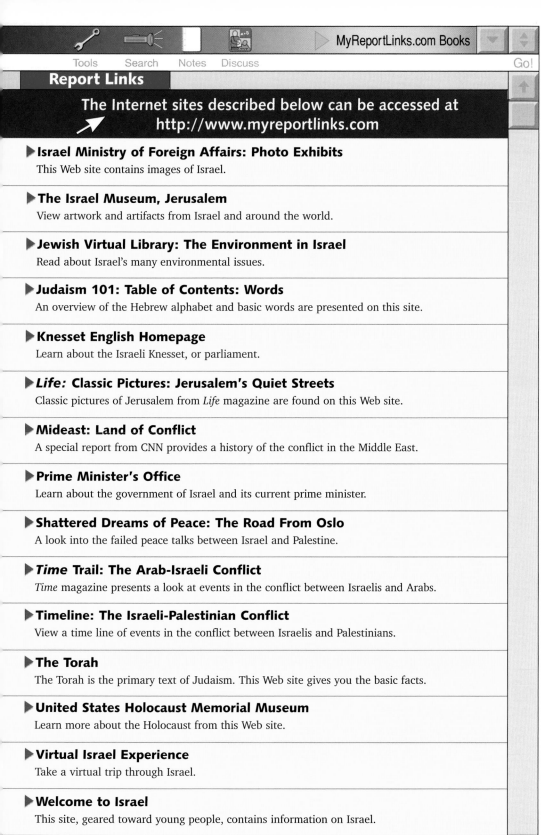
The Internet sites described below can be accessed at http://www.myreportlinks.com

▶**Israel Ministry of Foreign Affairs: Photo Exhibits**
This Web site contains images of Israel.

▶**The Israel Museum, Jerusalem**
View artwork and artifacts from Israel and around the world.

▶**Jewish Virtual Library: The Environment in Israel**
Read about Israel's many environmental issues.

▶**Judaism 101: Table of Contents: Words**
An overview of the Hebrew alphabet and basic words are presented on this site.

▶**Knesset English Homepage**
Learn about the Israeli Knesset, or parliament.

▶*Life:* **Classic Pictures: Jerusalem's Quiet Streets**
Classic pictures of Jerusalem from *Life* magazine are found on this Web site.

▶**Mideast: Land of Conflict**
A special report from CNN provides a history of the conflict in the Middle East.

▶**Prime Minister's Office**
Learn about the government of Israel and its current prime minister.

▶**Shattered Dreams of Peace: The Road From Oslo**
A look into the failed peace talks between Israel and Palestine.

▶*Time* **Trail: The Arab-Israeli Conflict**
Time magazine presents a look at events in the conflict between Israelis and Arabs.

▶**Timeline: The Israeli-Palestinian Conflict**
View a time line of events in the conflict between Israelis and Palestinians.

▶**The Torah**
The Torah is the primary text of Judaism. This Web site gives you the basic facts.

▶**United States Holocaust Memorial Museum**
Learn more about the Holocaust from this Web site.

▶**Virtual Israel Experience**
Take a virtual trip through Israel.

▶**Welcome to Israel**
This site, geared toward young people, contains information on Israel.

aliyah—A migration of Jews to Israel.

anti-Semitism—Hatred, prejudice, discrimination, and/or oppression against Jews or Judaism.

Ashkenazic Jews—Jews who hail from Europe.

atonement—Making up for an offense.

covenant—A binding agreement.

First and Second Temples—Sacred temples to God built by the Israelites/Jews in Jerusalem during ancient times.

Holocaust—The genocide of approximately 6 million European Jews and other peoples by the Nazis and their collaborators from 1933 to 1945.

intifada—A Palestinian uprising.

kashrut—Jewish dietary laws derived from the Book of Leviticus.

kibbutz—A farming community of Jewish Israelis in which people share property, responsibilities, and work.

Knesset—The legislative branch of the Israeli government.

kosher—Food prepared according to Jewish dietary laws. Also, the following of these laws.

Messiah—The expected king of the Jews.

moshav—A settlement of farms in Israel. Individuals own their own property, but work is organized collectively.

Orthodox Jews—Members of the most traditional branch of Judaism. They adhere to a strict interpretation of Jewish law and customs.

Palestinian Authority (PA)—The Palestinian governing body that oversees Palestinian territory in the West Bank and Gaza.

Palestine Liberation Organization (PLO)—A onetime terrorist organization that is now considered a legitimate political body. Its mission is to create a nation-state for the displaced Palestinians.

Palestinians—Arabs with roots to the land that is now Israel, the West Bank, Gaza, and the Golan Heights.

Sephardic Jews—Jews who are from the Middle East, North Africa, Spain, and the Mediterranean region.

Shabbat—The Jewish sabbath (day of rest), which lasts from sundown Friday to sundown Saturday.

suicide bomber—A terrorist who blows up himself or herself in order to kill or injure other people.

Torah—The five books of Moses, which are also the first five books of the Bible: Genesis, Exodus, Leviticus, Numbers, and Deuteronomy.

ultra-Orthodox Jews—Those who adhere to the most theologically conservative form of Judaism.

Wailing Wall—The only remaining wall from the kingdom of Israel's Second Temple, which was destroyed by the Romans in A.D. 70. Also called the Western Wall.

yarmulke—A skullcap worn by some Jewish males during times of worship (and by some Jews at all times).

Zionism—The movement dedicated to establishing a Jewish homeland in Palestine.

Chapter 1. Another Chance for Peace

1. "Leaders gather in Egypt for Arafat's funeral," *CNN.com*, November 11, 2004, <http://www.cnn.com/2004/WORLD/meast/11/11/arafat.main/> (June 18, 2005).

2. "Abbas offers hand of peace to Israel," *The Daily Star*, January 11, 2005, <http://www.dailystar.com.lb/article.asp?edition_id=10&categ_id=2&article_id=11723> (June 18, 2005).

3. Author interview with Donya Meijer, April 28, 2005.

4. Ken Ellingwood, "Hope for peace between Palestinians, Israelis at highest point since '93," *baltimoresun.com*, February 9, 2005, <http://www.baltimoresun.com/news/nationworld/bal-te.analysis09feb09,1,7378321.story?coll=bal-nationworld-utility> (June 18, 2005).

Chapter 2. Land and Climate

1. Harold M. Schulweis, "Israel: The Land and the Therapy," *Rabbi Harold Schulweis Archives*, n.d., <http://www.vbs.org/rabbi/hshulw/israel_bot.htm> (April 15, 2005).

2. Author interview with Meir Brooks, April 22, 2005.

3. Author interview with Meir Fishburn, April 25, 2005.

4. "Plague of Locusts Descends Upon Israel," *FOXNews.com*, November 22, 2004, <http://www.foxnews.com/story/0,2933,139282,00.html> (May 9, 2005).

5. Author interview with Meir Fishburn, April 25, 2005.

6. Author interview with Naomi Leitner, April 22, 2005.

Chapter 3. The Jewish Faith

1. Daphna Baram, "The defeat of the pork-eaters," *New Statesman,* December 6, 2004, <http://www.findarticles.com/p/articles/mi_m0FQP/is_4717_133/ai_n8586107> (April 12, 2005).

2. Will Durant, *The Story of Civilization VI. The Reformation* (New York: Simon and Schuster, 1957), p. 422.

3. David J. Hogan, editor-in-chief, *The Holocaust Chronicle* (Lincolnwood, Ill.: Publications International, 2001), pp. 41–42.

4. Author interview with Naomi Leitner, April 22, 2005.

5. Ibid.

6. Author interview with Meir Brooks, April 22, 2005.

7. Author interview with Shelley Yachbesh, April 27, 2005.

Chapter 4. Israeli Culture

1. Author interview with Naomi Leitner, April 22, 2005.

2. Author interview with Shelley Yachbesh, April 27, 2005.

3. Author interview with Donya Meijer, April 28, 2005.

4. Author interview with Jonah Schiffmiller, April 29, 2005.

5. Author interview with Shelley Yachbesh, April 27, 2005.

6. Author interview with Meir Brooks, April 22, 2005.

7. Author interview with Donya Meijer, April 28, 2005.

8. Ibid.

9. Author interview with Naomi Leitner, April 22, 2005.

10. Author interview with Burton Ravins, April 21, 2005.

11. Author interview with Meir Fishburn, April 25, 2005.

12. Author interview with Naomi Leitner, April 22, 2005.

13. Author interview with Meir Brooks, April 22, 2005.

Chapter 5. A Stateless People

1. David J. Hogan, editor-in-chief, *The Holocaust Chronicle* (Lincolnwood, Ill.: Publications International, 2001), p. 22.

2. U.S. Library of Congress, "Political Zionism," *Country Studies US,* n.d., <http://countrystudies .us/israel/9.htm> (May 4, 2005).

3. "Judaism and the Holy Land," *Holyland Resources,* n.d., <http://www.holylandalternatives .net/judaism.html> (May 6, 2005).

4. "Christian History & Biography," *ChristianityToday.com*, 1994–2005, <http://www.ctlibrary.com/4325> (September 27, 2005).

5. Winston Churchill, *The Nizkor Project,* n.d., <http://www.nizkor.org/ftp.cgi/orgs/american/oregon/ftp.py?orgs/american/oregon/banished.cpu/lies/lie.04> (May 9, 2005).

Chapter 6. An Embattled Nation

1. Author interview with Meir Brooks, April 22, 2005.

Chapter 7. A Strained Economy

1. Central Intelligence Agency, "Map & Graph: Military: Expenditures: Dollar figure," as reposted at *nationmaster.com*, n.d., <http://www.nationmaster.com/graph-T/mil_exp_dol_fig_cap> (June 2, 2005).

2. Author interview with Shelley Yachbesh, April 27, 2005.

3. Author interview with Naomi Leitner, April 22, 2005.

4. Author interview with Mitchell Bard, March 22, 2005.

5. Author interview with Meir Brooks, April 22, 2005.

6. Author interview with Mitchell Bard, March 22, 2005.

7. Ibid.

8. John Dobosz, "Israeli Stocks Heat Up As

Conflict Cools," *Forbes.com*, February 24, 2005, <http://www.forbes.com/investmentnewsletters/20 05/02/24/cz_jd_0224watch_inl.html> (May 21, 2005).

9. Author interview with Shelley Yachbesh, April 27, 2005.

10. Author interview with Naomi Leitner, April 22, 2005.

Altman, Linda Jacobs. *Impact of the Holocaust.* Berkeley Heights, N.J.: Enslow Publishers, Inc., 2004.

Charing, Douglas. *Judaism.* New York: DK Publishing, 2003.

Corona, Laurel. *Israel.* San Diego: Lucent Books, 2003.

Garfinkle, Adam. *Israel.* Philadelphia: Mason Crest Publishers, 2004.

Gunderson, Cory. *The Israeli-Palestinian Conflict.* Edina, Minn.: Abdo & Daughters, 2004.

Hayhurst, Chris. *Israel's War of Independence.* New York: Rosen Publishing Group, 2004.

Hogan, David J., editor-in-chief. *The Holocaust Chronicle.* Lincolnwood, Ill.: Publications International, 2000.

Katz, Samuel M. *Jerusalem or Death: Palestinian Terrorism.* Minneapolis: Lerner Publishing Group, 2004.

King, John. *Israel and Palestine.* Chicago: Raintree, 2005.

United Nations. *The Search for Peace in the Middle East.* New York: United Nations Publications, 2003.

Wagner, Heather Lehr. *Israel and the Arab World.* Philadelphia: Chelsea House Publishers, 2002.